The Leadership Strategy of Jesus

# ENDORSEMENTS

"Rich Halcombe has encouraged literally thousands of pastors over the course of his amazing career. I've known Rich for over thirty-five years. We both pastored small dysfunctional churches after seminary and would routinely call and encourage each other with our crazy stories. I've watched Rich preach to thousands as the Teaching Pastor of a large mega-church, and I've seen him speak life to fellow ministers one-on-one. Over the years, he has lived out the principles of this *The Leadership Strategy of Jesus* as an influencer, a church planter, a pastor, and a pastor of pastors. His humility, humor, relatability, and his ability to communicate the timeless principles of Jesus into our hectic modern reality make *The Leadership Strategy of Jesus* a must-read for anyone in leadership."

—**Dr. Mark Shook**, Founding Pastor,
Community of Faith

"The concepts found in *The Leadership Strategy of Jesus* that Dr. Rich Halcombe uses are transformative for leaders and organizations. Our healthcare and education companies have worked with him for the past three years, and all aspects of our business have benefited from the wisdom and strategies that he brings with a Christian perspective that is relevant to marketplace advancement. I recommend *The Leadership Strategy of Jesus* and am thankful for the author's impact on our organizations and me."

—**Tim Robinson**, CEO,
Addiction Recovery Care

"Rich possesses a rare combination of academic knowledge and practical wisdom that, together, forms his uniquely valuable, insightful perspectives on how Jesus would have us apply His teachings to our modern lives. Whatever Rich writes, you should read: You'll learn much, and he'll provide a practical framework by which you can improve your life and everyone around you."

—**Clark Harvey**, Executive Director,
Brighter Days Foundation

"Every great company has a mission, and every great CEO develops a strategy to lead employees to achieve it. Rich Halcombe has captured the essence of Jesus's strategy and has written a must-read reference for anyone who wants to live life to the fullest, for any leader that yearns for their organization to have meaningful impact and influence, and for any group of individuals working together for God's purpose."

—**Paul D. McKinney,**
CEO and Chairman of the Board,
Ring Energy, Inc.

"In the age of the spontaneous, few have the courage to understand that without a strategy and effective approach to implementing a vision, it will never become a reality. Rich Halcombe has done just that. Having him set teams, churches, and organizations free to live out their dream, there is none better than the counsel and advice that Rich offers in *The Leadership Strategy of Jesus*. I highly recommend this new work to any leader or team serious about seeing a vision become a reality."

—**Terry Walling,**
President, Leader Breakthru

"Every leader I know longs to be effective. But what does that mean, and how do we get there? This is what Rich Halcombe helps church leaders with in his book *The Leadership Strategy of Jesus*. So many in the church today are taking their leadership cues from the secular workplace and business world. Rich goes straight to the life of Jesus to help us discover why his model of personal and organizational strategy is the best path to take. If you are a pastor or church leader and looking for some direction on how to best lead yourself and your organization, *The Leadership Strategy of Jesus* is for you. Read it, implement its instruction, and watch what God does in your life and church."

—**Jarrett Stephens**, Senior Pastor,
Champion Forest Baptist Church,
Author, *The Always God: He Hasn't Changed and You're Not Forgotten*

"Dr. Halcombe possesses an innate ability to observe situations and see opportunities where most of us only see difficulties. You will find *The Leadership Strategy of Jesus* a Christ-centered, biblical approach to help us know what 'to do' and 'what not to do,' which has been called 'the essence of strategy.' These ancient principles with contemporary applications would be effective in Fortune 500 board rooms or the planning sessions of the local church."

—**Mitch Webb**, Executive Director,
Huntington City Mission

"I've heard Dallas Willard discuss the utmost brilliance of Jesus as an overlooked portion of His nature. We certainly see Jesus as being the humble servant but don't spend much time contemplating His genius. Rich Halcombe is a leader who displays to anyone who gets close to him that brilliance and servanthood are not mutually exclusive and are the hallmarks of Christ's work in his life. Rich oversees and leads north of 140+ churches, of which I am one. His combination of high-level thinking and servanthood makes him arguably the most potent voice I know when it comes to putting theology and strategy into action. I would not be in a position of leadership like I am if Rich Halcombe didn't serve and lead me the way he has. Any word he shares, any idea or strategy he speaks of or sees as crucial to the life and ministry of Jesus is worth learning about. He will humbly serve anyone who listens, and his knowledge can take the young leader or the seasoned pastor to the utmost heights of any ministry endeavor."

—**Joel Kovacs**, Lead Pastor,
Five14 Church

"Rich is not just one of the kindest men I know and the most knowledgeable about Scripture, but he is also one of the most effective at turning around struggling organizations, bringing people together to accomplish a common goal, and assessing and developing talent—in other words, leading."

—**Ellen Cathey**, Officer, Fortune 100 company,
Founder, Christian Professional Women's Forum

"In his book *The Leadership Strategy of Jesus*, Dr. Rich Halcombe answers many of the biggest questions that all too frequently arise in churches and organizations during times of struggle. He methodically walks through the principles that Christ Himself modeled for effectively leading, planning, organizing, and working through others. Rich's unique ability to teach meaningful concepts in simple, relatable, and retainable ways will no doubt benefit pastors, team leaders, lay leaders, and Christian businesspeople alike."

—**R. Scott Fenter**, Director,
In-Store Experience and Innovation, Jared Jewelry

"Some leaders have a God-given ability to cast a vision that is clear and compelling. Other leaders have been blessed by God with the knowledge and experience to articulate and execute a strategy that will have a significant impact on the kingdom of God. Few leaders excel in both vision casting and strategy development. Dr. Rich Halcombe has proven to be one of those rare leaders who excel in both. I have been blessed for over fifteen years to have the opportunity to grow through the wisdom, teaching, and support of Dr. Rich. Now you have that same opportunity through the study of Dr. Rich's book *The Leadership Strategy of Jesus*."

—**Jim Dreisbach**, Sr. Director,
Human Resources Global Operations, Intentional Interim Pastor

"Dr. Rich Halcombe is an accomplished leader, educator, and theologian who has a passion for equipping and motivating others to be better leaders by providing biblically based direction and clarity. Rich's background, experience, and organizational skills provide the foundation for his effectiveness, but it is his love, compassion, and missionary-driven purpose that truly sets him apart. Rich has successfully demonstrated that the strategies of Jesus continue to develop Christian leaders and grow congregations to achieve impactful results for His Kingdom."

—**Mark Armstrong**, Texas

"Rich is one of the best leaders and teachers of strategy that I have known. He has great knowledge of Scripture, a heart to serve, and a love for Jesus. Rich is a visionary with the unique ability to write about Christ's strategy in leadership and service. Christ had a specific vision, and *The Leadership Strategy of Jesus* encapsulates this vision of how Christ led and served while on earth."

—**Kelli Karlich**, Executive Director,
Stowe Mission of Central Ohio

"So grateful for Rich Halcombe's leadership in my life. He has strategically pulled things out from within to help me recognize and step into my calling. His tools to help me ponder direction in my personal and professional life have been monumentally centering. Any time in the mind of Rich Halcombe is truly a treasure."

—**Travis Whittaker**, Lead Pastor,
Mile City Church

"Church leaders are always looking for ways to impact their community. However, most of us don't know where to start. *The Leadership Strategy of Jesus* will encourage you to think biblically and strategically about your leadership and the local church. Dr. Rich Halcombe loves the church and its leader, and his insights will inspire you to not only grow yourself but also the Kingdom of God."

—**Daniel Lucas**, Senior Pastor,
Better Life Church

"*The Leadership Strategy of Jesus* is a refreshing, insightful, biblical, and helpful tool for any leader who understands the importance of strategy. It is rare to find a resource that is rooted in the Scripture with practical handles on every page. Dr. Halcombe loves leaders with the heart of Jesus and wants them to succeed. He has taught our church leadership team these principles for years, and we still reap the benefits regularly. Pastor, this is the book you have always thought should be written. It will be a great help to your ministry."

—**Steve Griffith**, Senior Pastor,
Osborne Baptist Church

"Rich Halcombe is the team builder extraordinaire. His gift for leading strategically is nothing short of amazing. Knowing Rich, I can't think of anyone more qualified than he to write a book about leading as Jesus led!"

—**Lezlie Armour**, Missions Minister,
Champion Forest Baptist Church

"It is a privilege to recommend *The Leadership Strategy of Jesus* by my good friend Dr. Rich Halcombe. It will help pastors, staff members, and church leaders alike understand the biblical principles of church health and church growth. This well-written book will challenge, convict, inspire, and encourage. I am looking forward to discussing it with my staff as we apply it to our church."

—**Dr. Jeff Schreve**, Pastor,
First Baptist Church Texarkana and From Him Heart Ministries

"I had the privilege of engaging with *The Leadership Strategy of Jesus* through his leadership cohorts, and the content changed my leadership within our church plant. It allowed me to strategically think through the systems and structures used by our church to bring better alignment across our ministries. If you are looking for a resource that will challenge you personally and bring a more cohesive strategy to your church or organization, I would highly recommend you read and utilize *The Leadership Strategy of Jesus!*"

—**Aaron Taylor**, Teaching Pastor,
Living Hope Church

"Rich Halcombe is a hugely effective kingdom leader. His current ministry is literally erupting in expansion and impact. His latest book, *The Leadership Strategy of Jesus*, is a powerful tool for those of us who aspire to lead more effective ministries. It has been forged on the anvil of Rich's thirty years of leadership and fleshed out through his coaching pastors and churches to greater effectiveness. Like Rich, it is accessible, clear, direct, practical, spiritual, and hugely helpful. Buy it! Read it! Do it!"

—**Dr. Dave Earley**, Founder, Dave Earley Ministries,
Lead Pastor, First Baptist Church of Grove City, Ohio,
Associate Professor, Liberty University Divinity School

"In the book *The Leadership Strategy of Jesus*, Dr. Rich Halcombe accurately captures the essence of Jesus's approach to the church and its leadership. Trust me when I say that he is speaking from a heart of a warrior who has been in the trenches with many struggling leaders—this was NOT a book written from an ivory tower! On the contrary, Rich embodies every one of the principles espoused in it. If you want to grow as a leader and if you want your church to flourish, I highly recommend reading *The Leadership Strategy of Jesus!*"

—**Dr. David A. Wheeler**, Professor of Evangelism,
Liberty University Rawlings School of Divinity,
Sr. Executive Director, Liberty University Shepherd

"Having known Dr. Halcombe for several years and been through the leader-INCREASE cohort, I can say with truth and confidence that Rich is one of the greatest leaders I know. Not only does he lead well, but he develops leaders with passion and commitment to see them become great leaders themselves. I have no doubt you will grow as a leader and be blessed by *The Leadership Strategy of Jesus.*"

—**Austin Mathis**, Church Planter, Grace Church

# THE
# LEADERSHIP
# STRATEGY
## OF JESUS

*Living Intentionally in Ministry & Life*

# DR. RICH HALCOMBE

NASHVILLE

NEW YORK • LONDON • MELBOURNE • VANCOUVER

# The Leadership Strategy of Jesus

## Living Intentionally in Ministry and Life

Published in New York, New York, by Morgan James Publishing. Morgan James is a trademark of Morgan James, LLC. www.MorganJamesPublishing.com

Proudly distributed by Ingram Publisher Services.

All Scripture quotations, unless otherwise indicated, are taken from the Holy Bible, New International Version®, NIV®. Copyright ©1973, 1978, 1984, 2011 by Biblica, Inc.™ Used by permission of Zondervan. All rights reserved worldwide. www.zondervan.com. The "NIV" and "New International Version" are trademarks registered in the United States Patent and Trademark Office by Biblica, Inc.™

**Morgan James BOGO™**

A **FREE** ebook edition is available for you or a friend with the purchase of this print book.

_____

CLEARLY SIGN YOUR NAME ABOVE

**Instructions to claim your free ebook edition:**
1. Visit MorganJamesBOGO.com
2. Sign your name CLEARLY in the space above
3. Complete the form and submit a photo of this entire page
4. You or your friend can download the ebook to your preferred device

ISBN 9781636980362 paperback
ISBN 9781636980379 ebook
Library of Congress Control Number:
2022944359

**Cover & Interior Design by:**
Christopher Kirk
www.GFSstudio.com

Morgan James is a proud partner of Habitat for Humanity Peninsula and Greater Williamsburg. Partners in building since 2006.

Get involved today! Visit MorganJamesPublishing.com/giving-back

*For all pastors and business leaders who want to make an impact with their lives . . .*
*and enjoy seeing God do what only God can do.*

# TABLE OF CONTENTS

# ACKNOWLEDGMENTS

To my wife, Tina, whose grace, beauty, and godliness make every day nicer. To Damon Shook, who taught me more about leadership than any other one person. He showed me you can lead an incredibly effective church as well as an amazing family.

To Denny Taylor, a godly man who spent countless hours instilling in me what he learned as the manager of Continuous Performance Improvement at one of the world's largest companies.

To Mom and Dad, who built a godly foundation into my life and loved our local church.

To my brothers, Jim, Bob, Davy, and Donnie.

To the following generations, Richard, Samantha, Nichole, Zac, Luke, Eli, Magnolia, and Huck.

To Mandy and Shelby, who make everything I do better.

To Karen Anderson and Morgan James Publishing, without whose help this dream would not have become a reality.

# INTRODUCTION

## Why Are Some Churches Thriving While Others Are Dying—When They All Love Jesus?

We know Jesus effectively accomplished His mission and continues to achieve it.

After all, the church is the largest organization in history, with approximately 2.4 billion adherents.[1] The local bride of Christ, the church, outnumbers every country, company, and nonprofit organization on the planet that has ever existed. The church exists in all 197 countries of the world. Some countries sport massive cathedrals and sprawling complexes, while others force the church underground.

Nevertheless, the church is still there worshiping, discipling, and evangelizing. Different languages, continents, and cultures all find expressions of the person and work of Christ. It's mind-blowing to think it started with Jesus of Nazareth and His first followers.

With this being the case, why are so many churches struggling and ineffective?

I have come to believe they don't understand or follow Jesus's leadership strategy.

In my decades on the planet, I have been involved with churches on virtually every level of leadership. I grew up in the church and began my ministry serving in a small, rural church. I continued serving as senior staff of a church averaging 4,500 in attendance weekly on one campus.

I've seen and worked the inner workings (the good, the bad, and the ugly). I have been part of the committees looking for a pastor, watched churches trying to figure out what to do, and led several, either as pastor, associate pastor, or interim pastor. I've directed a growing network that now numbers over 140 churches.

With a few exceptions, most churches seem to struggle to make an impact in their local setting. From my earliest years in ministry, I was curious to understand why this was true.

## From Calling to Leading

When I first became a pastor at twenty-six, I knew how to teach the Bible. But I had no idea how to lead an organization. In fact, I didn't even know I was supposed to know how to lead an organization. Two weeks after becoming a pastor, I realized my church was in trouble. Twenty-five years of steady decline preceded my arrival. From the time I started my role as pastor, I worked hours and hours every week studying, preaching, praying, witnessing, and visiting the sick and those in nursing homes. But none of it stemmed the decline. Despite all the work, we only had a few visitors to the church and only one family over the course of three years ever became members.

I never felt depressed until I became a pastor. Maybe I wasn't clinically depressed in that first church, but for an active guy to spend all morning in bed staring at the ceiling, I knew something was bad. My mood didn't shift much when I sat at my desk the rest of that day staring at the wall.

To get a boost of confidence, I drove to a local Christian university to hear a well-respected megachurch pastor who also wrote many biblical commentaries. I read and used several of his commentaries in preparing my messages. I was eager to see some newfound pastor friends and hear a great message on how I could improve the situation at church, maybe even figure out how to reverse the decline. The commentary-writing preacher basically told us that day, "If you preach the Bible correctly, God will build your church."

My heart sank. The hour-long drive home gave his words time to sink in. My church was dying a slow, painful death. With my two master's degrees from (at that time) the world's largest seminary and my fifteen or so hours of weekly sermon prep, I thought I did preach the Bible correctly. I even used that speaker's commentaries!

After all my years of preparation and hard work to become a pastor, it turns out, according to that guy, I could not even do the one thing I thought I could do. I wasn't a great preacher, but I was always prepared and stuck to the biblical text. So, obviously, the problem must be me. I wasn't enough. I just didn't have what it takes, whatever that is. How can I be such a failure in something I felt called to do?

To make matters worse, my growing little family depended on the church going well. Pastoring was not only my calling; it also provided for my wife and kids financially. The church was also our social circle. Since we were new to Columbus, Ohio, the people in the church were also our only friends. Even more encompassing, the church was my career and my spiritual support. It felt as if my whole life would go down the tube if the church did not turn around.

So, what were my choices? Go to another church? What other church in the world would hire a no-name pastor from a "dead" church? I felt like I needed to do something. So, I hand-addressed and mailed my résumé to every state office in our denomination . . . with no replies. As I sat in my "Pastor's Office" (the sign on my door), I saw my undergraduate degree hanging on the wall. It read "Industrial Arts Technology Management." While my degree didn't align with the calling I felt I'd been given by God, I realized I needed to do something drastic.

So, I drove to the local IBEW (International Brotherhood of Electrical Workers) union hall, where electricians got trained. But sitting in the parking lot, I couldn't get out of the car. I wanted to. My responsibility for my family pushed me to. Yet, something kept me in that seat.

Maybe it was just the electrical profession holding me back. After all, I'm not a detailed, step-by-step thinker, and that can (literally) kill you as an electrician. So, I pulled out the Yellow Pages to see how to become a plumber. It's good work, and I've never heard of a plumber getting killed if the pipes don't go together the right way. But I couldn't make myself pick up the phone to make the call.

During that same time frame, I decided to check out the medical profession, so I drove to the Mount Carmel School of Nursing. Maybe being a nurse would be my profession. After all, nurses help lots of people. Yet, inside I knew it wasn't my calling either.

In all the frustration and discouragement, the one thing I did know was that God called me to ministry. The weight of that calling outweighed everything else.

But even though I knew I was called, I still didn't know what to do. If I felt so worthless, confused, frustrated, and at times angry, maybe I wasn't the only one?

Those early years drove me to figure it out. I deliberately set out to study how churches and nonprofit organizations and businesses succeed. Since I had learned so little about what makes an organization go well in seminary, I looked everywhere I could. I attended seminars (both secular and sacred), read books, and interviewed leaders.

I eventually found the best answer in the pages of Scripture—through looking at Jesus's life and ministry through the lens of strategy.

## Why Many Churches Struggle Even When They Are Committed to Christ

Though it's impossible to know the exact number, suffice it to say I've personally worked with thousands of church leaders. Most of them are senior leaders in their churches. Others serve as staff ministers or lay leaders. After having led, mentored, coached, and discipled thousands of leaders, several similarities emerge:

→ **They all love Jesus.** Ask any one of them (and I have), and they will tell you they love the Lord and want to serve Him. This love for Jesus isn't just lip service. You can see it in their lives. After all, they invest their lives in service to Him. Many people say they follow Christ. These folks jumped in neck deep.

→ **They all want to do a good job.** I have yet to meet a single leader/staff or lay leader who wanted to do a poor job. Each of them wanted to excel at their task because they know what they do reflects on them personally. But they also wanted to help people. They believe in what the church does, and they want things in their church to go well.

→ **They are sincere.** You may hear stories of flimflam preachers who are "just in it for the money." In over three decades of vocational ministry, I've never met one. The women and men I know are dedicated people who serve in their churches because they want to help other people spiritually, emotionally, physically, and intellectually.

→ **They work hard.** Most of them work a lot of hours each week at their churches: more than they should in a lot of cases. These leaders facilitate meetings, counsel people in distress, feed the poor, study for and teach Bible studies, maintain the property, visit, pray, call, email, organize, lead, type, help, and serve others in numerous ways.

So, if church leaders want to love Jesus, do a good job, are sincere, and work hard, why don't churches do better? Why are so many churches dying and declining?

They don't understand Jesus's *strategy*.

Simply stated, strategy is a framework for getting from where you are to where you want to be.

Jesus possessed and embraced a personal strategy for life as well as an organizational strategy to lead the church, the body of Christ. Even though we aren't Jesus (there was only one begotten Son of God), we can use the same principles He used to lead effective businesses, churches, and nonprofit organizations.

Jesus demonstrated strategy in everything He did. His life wasn't random. *He did nothing by chance.*

---

### Strategy is a framework for getting from where you are to where you want to be.

---

And yet many of us in church leadership have been led to believe that "if we build it, they will come." This view stems from an underlying limiting belief that if our hearts are in the right place, we will have a thriving ministry.

But that then begs the question: Why doesn't everyone who loves Jesus have a thriving ministry?

In fact, it may surprise you to learn that the churches that reach and disciple lots of people or have major impact don't believe the Bible any more than those who don't.

Further, churches with major impact don't live more godly lives than others. They don't believe in better doctrine. They don't pray more. They aren't more sincere or hardworking or more genuine.

The churches that make major impact do so because they execute a God-honoring strategy. (By the way, that strategy includes believing the Bible, living godly lives, teaching good doctrine, praying, and being authentic.)

Truly effective churches use strategy the same way Jesus used strategy.

What if we look at Jesus's life and ministry from a different perspective—one of *intentionality*—in our plans and actions, not only in our hearts.

## What Suffers Without Jesus's Leadership Strategy?

If you don't execute a strategy like Jesus, what's at risk? What's the downside of just continuing to preach, teach, care, counsel, and nurture those in your congregation?

### The Pastor/Leader Suffers

In talking to church leaders who don't operate using a strategic rhythm of evaluation and implementation, I often hear things like, "Some things are going well, and some things aren't. I really don't know why." Another told me, "It just seems like I'm shooting in the dark. I don't know why we are getting results with some ministries and why other ministries flounder."

Lack of a strategy causes undue stress on a leader. What messages should you preach? What ministries should you start? What ministries lived out their useful life and need to end? How do you end a ministry? How can I handle the latest conflict?

This sampling of the never-ending self-questioning that leaders endure reveals the need for a comprehensive church strategy, owned and operated by all the leaders, not just the pastor. Without a strategy, leaders often feel a gnawing sense of unease because they aren't really sure what to do.

### The Congregation Suffers

It's not just the church leader who suffers. In churches that don't operate strategically, you find numerous gifted people who don't believe they fit. Since there's no real plan for the church, they don't see a way to contribute. Your church may complain about people not being involved. But if you don't provide a strategy for people to be involved, you disenable people to contribute.

For example, a woman who can lead a ministry will never volunteer if there is no new ministry to lead. Furthermore, she won't lead an existing ministry if the church has not built an on-ramp for her to get involved. Churches that don't use strategy suffer a deficit of volunteers and talent because there's no clear path for a gifted leader or volunteer to use her gifts.

## The Kingdom Suffers

That rural church where I came to know Christ helped my family in so many ways. They taught us about God and the Bible. The people loved us and provided food and clothes when we needed them.

All of us know that everybody needs love and truth. But if a church does not consciously provide a path for outsiders to become insiders, people outside the church suffer. People on the outside don't know they can find help inside the church. Probably the most painful consequence of the failure to execute an effective strategy is the lost opportunity for so many to live qualitatively different lives if there was an effective strategy in place.

---

*"As the devil showed great skill in tempting men to perdition, equal skill ought to be shown in saving them. The devil studied the nature of each man, seized upon the traits of his soul, adjusted himself to them, and insinuated himself gradually into his victims' confidence—suggesting splendors to the ambitious, gain to the covetous, delight to the sensuous, and a false appearance of piety to the pious—and a winner of souls ought to act in the same cautious and skillful way."*
*—Ignatius Loyola*

---

One of the great heartaches of my life is knowing, on a very personal level, the love, acceptance, and support people can find inside the church—but I also know those very same churches often don't operate intentionally so people from the outside *can get inside.*

Strategic churches reach more people because they intentionally plan, evaluate, and retool to make sure new people find a home.

*The Leadership Strategy of Jesus* includes everything (that's not hyperbole) you need to succeed in life and ministry. It starts with you, the leader. Then it includes the organization you lead. Your organization could be a church, an area within a church, a nonprofit organization, a company you direct, or even a department in a company. Although most of the applications of the principles in the book will be to church leadership, the principles introduced apply to all leaders in every vocation and organization. *The Leadership Strategy of Jesus* works if you work it. It encourages and gives direction to the hundreds of leaders I have personally coached. It can help you.

The great news is that when you apply a strategy like Jesus, you will be encouraged, energized even. Each day will provide a sense of peace and momentum, knowing all the bases are covered. In addition, you will feel good about fulfilling your calling. Oh sure, you'll still have some difficult days. Ministry is like that. But even on those difficult days, you'll possess an inner confidence knowing things are moving in the right direction. You can care for your family and, most importantly, fulfill God's call in a way that you will later hear, "Well done, good and faithful servant."

*The Leadership Strategy of Jesus* was written for you if you are a church leader and any of the following are true of you. You are:

→ Discouraged
→ Disheartened
→ Frustrated
→ Tired
→ Hurt
→ Confused about what works and what doesn't
→ Just not sure what to do next
→ Want to make greater kingdom impact

Because the great news is that when you apply a strategy like Jesus, you will be:

→ Encouraged
→ Restored
→ Optimistic
→ Edified
→ Enthusiastic

As a pastor, I've been where you are and experienced the struggles of leading a church—whether it's declining, stagnating, or growing rapidly.

In other words, I know your cup can overflow again with the reasons you went into ministry in the first place. At some point, we all come to the point where we say, "Restore unto me the joy of my salvation."

## Strategy Provides the Pathway

My unbending search for what to do as a pastor resulted in me later leading flourishing ministries in the next two churches, which ultimately *restored my joy in serving the church*. It has also guided me for the last two decades as I have led a network of churches to ever-increasing impact and influence.

The truth is few churches have a strategy to incorporate the whole of what they are supposed to be doing. Most don't have a well-considered strategy for what they already believe they should be doing! Church leaders often possess a rather vague sense of what should be happening and lack an overarching cohesive picture of how it all fits together.

Yes, they conduct worship services, preach, love people, disciple people, help the poor, share their faith, teach the Bible, and minister to their community. They see all the pieces but are missing the comprehensive picture of how it should look when all the pieces are in place. Furthermore, they don't know *why* the whole enterprise isn't growing and increasing its impact. They aren't even sure why they are effective in the areas they do well. Even worse, they don't know what to do about it.

The good news is *you can know*. Not only can you know, but you can also lead your church to greater effectiveness. Following Jesus's strategy makes clear how we need to lead the organization of the church. It systematically addresses each area within the church to evaluate and retool where needed. And it can restore not only your joy but the joy of those you serve.

The leadership strategy of Jesus works because Jesus *lived* it.

*Chapter 1*

# THE LEADERSHIP STRATEGY OF JESUS

*"Without a vision, the people perish."*
Proverbs 29:18

I believe this verse to be true, and I've seen it reveal itself as true. However, in my journey, I have also come to realize that *without a strategy, the vision perishes.*

## Is Jesus Picking Winners and Losers?

Does Jesus want some people and churches to succeed and others to fail? Is it that God only chooses certain ministries to be effective, and the rest of us are destined to flounder or worse? A lot of church leaders I know think this. But it's not true.

It is a mistake to think and say that "Jesus builds the church" and conclude we have nothing to do with it. In actuality, Jesus said "I will build my church" to His group of leaders who actually led the initiative. He then told them, "I will give you the keys to the kingdom" (Matthew 16:19).

The truth is we have a lot to do with the effectiveness of ministries. That's why God put us here. God did not create us to spectate what He does. God created us to trust Him and to move things forward as much as humanly possible. While we do what we can, He does what we can't. **No, Jesus is not picking winners and losers.** The reality is effective leaders embrace a strategy that absolutely includes relying on God.

Ineffective leaders, on the other hand, overestimate what God is supposed to do and underestimate what they are supposed to do. While ineffective leaders hope God will bless their ministries, effective leaders develop and implement a strategy to get the results they believe God wants.

To go a step further and give some thought about how a strategy is effectively implemented, let's review an example of how one was used to accomplish the goals of a giant, well-known evangelical organization.

## Billy Graham's Crusade

*An illustration of how strategy was used to attract a large crowd of followers.*

In the early 1990s, the name Billy Graham filled stadiums across this country and the world. At least, that's what I thought before I helped with a crusade. As it turns out, Billy Graham's name did not fill stadiums. His strategy did.

Let's take a closer look at what that means. At the request of several local pastors, the Billy Graham Crusade conducted a crusade in Columbus, Ohio, in September 1993. I often thought, and I'm guessing many people thought, Billy Graham's name and reputation brought in the masses. You see the billboards, hear the radio and television advertisements, and a whole lot of people go to hear Billy Graham. Thousands filled stadiums across the country when Billy Graham spoke.

But that's not really how it worked.

As an associate pastor for Dublin Baptist Church, we decided to take the youth to be trained as counselors for the people who responded during the crusade. The Billy Graham Crusade taught first-rate evangelism training, and I wanted our teens to benefit from it, and they did. I expected great training. Yet I didn't anticipate learning how they packed out those stadiums. Our training started in January 1993, eight months before the big stadium event with the musicians and Billy Graham preaching. Evangelism occupied a central place but was not the majority of the time invested. A large part of the crusade included training people in many churches to pray, serve, and invite their neighbors to the crusade. That's how you fill venues.

One of their leaders shared a statistic: *Ninety percent of the Billy Graham Crusade happens before the public stadium event.* That forethought required the execution of a decisive strategy.

From the outside looking in, I would have thought the stadium event would have been 90 percent of the crusade (if I put a percentage to it). Having worked for, in, and with churches for the last three decades, I would say it's probably the same for churches. Most of the effectiveness of churches comes from a strategy that includes praying, training, planning, delegating, and preparing. Note that all of those things happen before Sunday morning.

Like the Billy Graham Evangelistic Association, effective churches utilize organizational leadership and a sound strategy to achieve kingdom results.

Even with a globally recognizable name, those top leaders did not depend on reputation or publicity to get people there. Each church leader and person who attended training chose and prayed for three people, ministered to them, and invited them to the stadium for one of the crusade nights. In addition, each church leader received encouragement to lead each person in their church to do the same: pray for three people, minister to them, and invite them to one night of the crusade. Beyond that, a lot of work, strategic planning, meetings, praying, seeking God, and actions contributed to those five or so nights.

As church leaders, that begs the question, "What do we do to reach people?" The Billy Graham Association formulated and executed an organizational strategy the way Jesus did. Consequently, they saw thousands upon thousands come to Christ. So, why would church leaders think that churches don't need a strategy to lead a church?

## The Church is Unique

The leadership strategy of Jesus can position any organization to be impactful and influential. It transforms and improves the operation of businesses, nonprofits, and churches. The strategy of Jesus works. It works for organizations and individuals, leaders and non-leaders, and even you and me. Yet, it's important for us to remember the church differs from every other organization on the planet. Understanding the unique nature and functioning of the church is key to achieving kingdom results in a ministry setting.

Truth be told, you'll find Christian leaders inside many organizations. They lead the C-Suite, possess departmental oversight, or maintain and support other business functions. Yet, these businesses or nonprofit organizations don't take their charter from the pages of Scripture. Nonprofit and for-profit organizations don't solely commit to Christ's purposes the way the church does. Those companies and non-profits certainly perform vital functions for us as human beings. But their primary interests lie outside being Christ's body. They manufacture products we need, provide services, and perform mercy ministries. These are all good and necessary.

Yet, the church stands alone as the one organization of like-minded people who follow God as an entire entity. Although there may be some exceptions, people work in the local church because they love God, follow Him, and want others to do likewise.

In addition, the church is the one institution Jesus Himself created and led. "I will build my church," He said. Although Jesus Christ can bless and honor any organization, He only personally identifies with the church, and he calls the church "the Bride[2] of Christ." The church, and the church alone, is wed to Christ. (That's also the reason we use the feminine personal pronoun to describe her.)

The Bible also tells us the church is "His body" (Colossians 1:24). No other entity occupies this space so closely identified to the Lord. The church, His body, and His bride stand uniquely because of Jesus's declaration, along with the fact He founded her. Her beginning and her purpose set the church apart from every other organization. Since this is true, it's all the more reason we should lead her the way He did. If you lead a church, know God uniquely called you for His kingdom purposes.

## What Is the Leadership Strategy of Jesus?

The leadership strategy of Jesus provides the pathway for anyone to live life to the fullest. When followed, the strategy encompasses and optimizes all of life. No matter your origin, identity, or culture, the strategy of Jesus involves the totality of who you are and the impact you make on those closest to you and on the world.

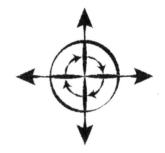

The leadership strategy of Jesus combines Jesus's personal and organizational strategies into one comprehensive whole. It encompasses all of you and gives you a roadmap to living a life of impact and peace. Before I discovered Jesus's strategy, I often wondered, *Am I missing something?* I worked hard, loved my family, studied, prayed, and followed Christ, but I could not get away from the gnawing feeling that there might be a key part of life I was somehow leaving out. The strategy of Jesus answered that question. Unquestionably, Jesus lived an incredible life of impact and peace. If I could figure out how He did it, I reasoned, it should work for me. It certainly has.

The leadership strategy of Jesus includes both the personal and the organizational. The Personal Strategy comes first. It's primary because your internal development precedes external impact. Decisions, as an example, are personal before they are organizational. Who you are on the inside regularly shows up in the life you live on the outside. As a leader, your personal beliefs, habits, thoughts, and attitudes directly impact everything in your organization. When you get better personally, your organization gets better. As you go, so goes your organization. Growing leaders lead growing organizations.

But don't make the mistake of thinking you only need to work on yourself. Many leaders miss God's best by believing this false assertion. As a leader, you definitely must work on yourself. But to be an effective leader, you must also work on the organization. You need to work "on" the church and not just work "in" the church.

We will examine all the major elements you need to lead your church effectively. I've used these key elements inside two different churches, as executive director of a network of churches, as the CEO of a nonprofit company, and as the owner of two for-profit companies as well as coaching hundreds of leaders from both the business and church worlds. The leadership strategy of Jesus works in every organization. We will see that Jesus not only led Himself personally but also led the church organizationally. For you to be an effective leader, you must also do both.

Here's a warning: Don't exclude Organizational Strategy. Too many people in general, and Christian leaders in particular, wrongly believe internal development somehow magically results in organizational health. It doesn't work like that. You definitely need to develop personally; just don't stop there. To be effective organizationally, there are additional skills you need to possess.

How do you improve personally? You work on yourself.

How do you improve your church? You work on the organization.

When both strategies (the personal and the organizational) work together and gain alignment, an incredible transformation occurs: You produce your greatest kingdom results. When you're clear on why you exist, are developing the elements of your personal life, align it with where you lead in any organization and work it, it all moves toward kingdom advancement.

It's like flipping a switch when you enter a room and the light goes on. You can see the light, but you also know it shines because of wires in the wall that you cannot see. An electrical system and structure support the switch.

One of the houses we bought as an investment property looked normal. You saw what you expected when you walked through each room: overhead light fixtures, light switches, and electrical outlets. But when you flipped a light switch, nothing happened. The lights did not come on even though all the visible parts were there. It's what you couldn't see that was the problem. Someone had stolen most of the internal electrical wires.

The switch on the wall and the light fixture were there, but nothing connected the two. (Fortunately, we knew this ahead of time. It helped us get a good deal on the property.) But it wasn't until my father-in-law and I rewired the house that the lights finally worked. We used the existing light switches and fixtures but just added the behind-the-scenes wiring to do what they were manufactured to do and light up the rooms.

Some leaders mistakenly believe all you need are the switches and the light fixtures. They get frustrated and wonder why the church isn't "working." Like an electrical system in a house, it might look good on the outside, but if key internal elements are missing, we won't get our desired results. The light won't come on.

In working with churches, almost without fail, it's this organizational piece that is lagging. Christian leaders know to do the personal work. They pray, preach, worship, evangelize, and disciple. But when they don't include the elements that actually build the organization, those churches produce lackluster results.

Jesus's leadership strategy included both the personal and the organizational elements. His strategy looks like this:

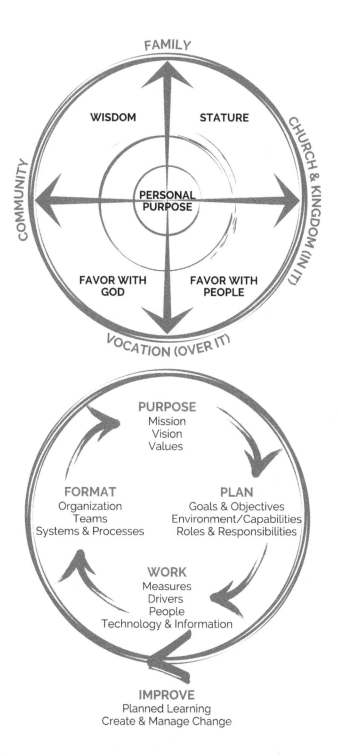

## Personal Strategy

*Grow in wisdom, stature, favor with God, and favor with people.*

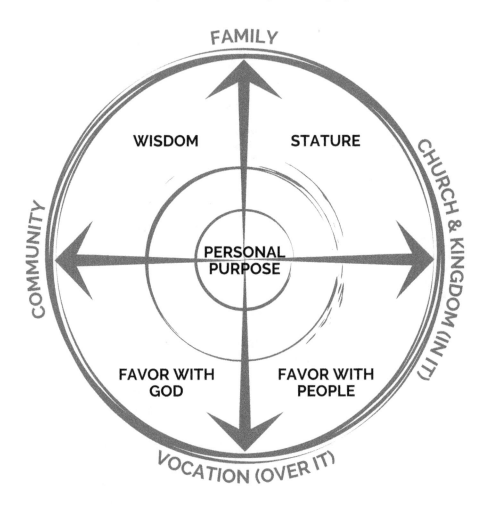

Jesus's personal purpose forms the centerpiece of His personal strategy, the first part of His overall leadership strategy. Jesus tells us why He came. He possessed crystal clarity about His personal purpose.

In John 14:6, Jesus Himself tells us, "I am the way, the truth, and the life. No one comes to the Father except through me." In Luke 19:10, Jesus, who described Himself as the Son of Man, told the listeners, "The Son of Man came to seek and to save the lost."

*Jesus came to redeem people. That was His personal purpose.*

Dr. W.A. Criswell, the longtime pastor of First Baptist Church in Dallas, Texas, called it the "Scarlet Thread through the Bible." That one theme wends its way through the sixty-six books of the Bible, written over a period of 1,500 years, penned by forty different authors on three different continents in three languages. Many different inputs, but the overarching purpose is solitary: the salvation of people. The Bible claims one purpose, and that purpose found its fulfillment in Christ. It was Jesus's personal purpose. *Then He used the church as the delivery system to accomplish His personal purpose.*

With His personal purpose clearly in place, the Bible tells us in Luke 2:52 that Jesus increased in four ways:

1. Wisdom (Mentally)
2. Stature (Physically)
3. Favor with God (Spiritually)
4. Favor with people (Socially/Emotionally)

What goes on *inside* the circle (Personal Purpose at the center and increasing in wisdom, stature, favor with God, favor with people) gives you skills to better live into your four personal domains *outside* the circle:

→ Family: the people you are related to
→ Church and Kingdom: your faith community
→ Community: the place where you "live"
→ Vocation: the organization you use to fulfill your personal purpose

All five elements inside the circle better the four domains outside the circle. For example, the more you grow in your favor with people, the better your familial relationships. Additionally, when your favor with God increases, you're more equipped to interact with and positively impact your community. As you increase all the elements inside the circle, you upgrade your impact on all the relationships outside the circle. *(Jesus's use of personal strategy is discussed in detail in chapter 6.)*

## My Early Misjudgment in Personal Strategy (My Story)

I thought my growing-up years would be enough character development to be effective in ministry. They were not. Those formidable years of abject poverty, trying to find my identity in a family with two special needs brothers and living in vastly different cultures, were simply the beginning.

I bounced around a lot as a child. I went to three schools in the third grade and then a fourth school in the fourth grade. In fact, during second grade, I was the only white boy in a predominantly black class outside the District of Columbia in Prince George's County, Maryland.

Here's my second-grade class:

I loved going to school and loved my friends. As is true with many children, particularly at that time, it seemed like adults focused on race, but we were just kids, and race didn't occur to us. It was only years later, when looking at pictures, that I even realized that I was the only white boy in my class. For me, it was just normal.

But then we left.

We moved from inside the Beltway in the District of Columbia to Appalachia to live with my mom's parents in Huntington, West Virginia. No sooner had I settled there and made new friends than we moved yet again. The constant introduction of new and different people into my life made it necessary to develop the skill of "Finding favor with *people*" (as mentioned above as one of the four ways required to develop personally). It would have been impossible to find new friends and fit in socially if I had not developed that skill.

The summer before my fourth-grade year, Mom and Dad bought a house in southern Ohio. It was a "fixer-upper" that never got fixed up. It was the builder's first house, and he had taken shortcuts that created significant problems from the get-go. And without money to make things right, that house only added another layer to an already difficult life.

The first night after we moved in, there was a torrential downpour. We managed to move everything inside, but the next morning, we watched as our unpacked boxes floated in six inches of water in the basement.

That was only the beginning.

One afternoon, as I got off the bus from school, I stumbled over a small hole in the ground. It was only about eight inches in diameter, and I had never noticed it before. I went into the house and told my mom, and when my dad came home from work, she showed him. In that short period of time, the hole had gotten even deeper.

Coming from living in the city, we had never heard the words septic tank before.

But we quickly discovered how awful septic problems could be!

Not having the money to pay a plumber, an army of men from church helped my dad dig eight feet down to the top of the collapsed septic tank. (Later, my folks discovered that the builder had installed the septic tank backward.) The team of men lifted bucket after bucket of dirt, hand over hand, flashlights pointed in the middle of a dark, cold night.

Even as a child, I saw times of devastation coupled with the grace of God's people. That was one of those times. I came to understand how carelessness (or greed, or inexperience) hurt innocent people but that the goodness of people could help to counteract the pain, even when it didn't resolve the problem.

My dad was a heavy equipment mechanic who worked hard at two jobs for most of his life. But even with those jobs, his income never kept up with all the family's needs.

To add to the mix, our family grew suddenly. I was eight years old and already had two younger brothers when my mom unexpectedly gave birth to twin boys.

Sadly, both of the twins (Davy and Donnie) were diagnosed as significantly developmentally delayed. My parents were told they would only function mentally at a one or two-year-old level. My folks devoted their lives to loving my brothers. As difficult as life was with a large family and twin boys with special needs, my dad always said he would never institutionalize them. They were his sons, and he was committed to doing everything he could to love them right where they were. It was a model of unconditional love that would stay with me my entire life.

My dad shared the twins' diagnosis with us when we pulled out of the grocery store parking lot one Sunday afternoon. He usually stopped at the store on the way home from church on Sundays. I think he was checking the prices since he always hunted for bargains.

On that Sunday, I was riding in the back seat with my four brothers, just like always. But on that particular day, as he was pulling away, he laid the news on us. "Boys," he said, "Your brothers have a permanent intellectual disability. They aren't just slow. The sooner you come to grips with that, the better off you'll be." Now, I knew Mom and Dad had taken the twins to get them tested at the Nisonger Center at Ohio State University. Mom and Dad knew something wasn't right with the twins' development. Well, we all did. The twins weren't talking, didn't understand simple things, and they screamed and ran around the house a lot. So, Mom and Dad drove them two and a half hours from home to find out why they behaved so erratically and their development was delayed. Profound intellectual disability was the answer.

Later, maybe it was because of the testing at OSU (I never really knew for sure), a couple of young women (we will call aides) from Marshall University came to the house and started working with the twins one summer. It was a behavior modification study. They (or Mom) would ask Donnie or Davy to do something simple. Something like, "Davy (or Donnie), please pick up the cup" (that he just knocked off the table). When neither of the twins did what they asked, one of the aides tried to sit one of them in time-out. Since the twins were three years old at the time, the aides thought sitting them in time-out for three minutes was appropriate.

I don't think either of the twins ever sat in that little chair for the entire three minutes. Sometimes one would last a few seconds, maybe even a minute occasionally. Most of the time, however, I remember them squirming, screaming, pulling away, and running. I don't remember them sitting very much. Finally, after several weeks and several attempts, the aides quit coming. It just didn't work out. But they weren't any more disappointed than my mom was. She and my dad tried everything they knew, but the twins still operated with minds and wills of their own. My dad and I used to wonder together what went on in their minds.

We also discovered that the twins were "hyperactive," to make matters worse. (I don't even remember where the term came from.) So, not only did they have low IQs, but now we knew why they screamed and yelled and ran and grabbed and knocked stuff off tables and made a big mess every time they ate. (That messy eating left my brother Jim and me with the job of major cleanup every night after dinner.)

Because of the twins' behavior and our lack of money, we seldom went out to eat. One of those times, all seven of us walked into a restaurant to get a seat. No sooner had we gotten in the door when Donnie threw himself on the floor and started kicking his feet and screaming. With even more significant special needs than Davy, Donnie had a hard time with most things in life. Going to a new place seemed to top the list of experiences that set him off. So, in the midst of the screaming and kicking, some lady sitting at a nearby table said to my mom, "If that were my son, I would spank him." That lady had no clue what my parents were dealing with every day of their lives. When she said that I don't remember if I was more embarrassed for myself or hurt for my mom and dad. So, after her comment, we scooped up Donnie and left the restaurant without sitting or eating.

The twins' hyperactivity didn't stop when the sun went down. As far as I know, my mom didn't sleep through the night for forty-some years. The twins were up every night. I was only mildly aware of this until years later when my dad died. When my dad passed, all of his living siblings came to town, along with my brothers Jim and Bob with their families and me with mine. Getting together with our extended family was a treasured time. They loved and accepted the twins just like we did. I don't remember a single instance when somebody in our family didn't care for and protect them. Even though we enjoyed seeing all those Halcombes, it was definitely a painful time after losing my dad. Yet, it was also a healing time with a bunch of people who loved and accepted each other just as they were. So, it was very sad when everybody had to go home. Most of them lived in the DC area, and Jim, Bob, and I lived in different states.

I could tell my mom was really struggling. So, after most of the family left, I had Mom stay with a friend for a night of respite. I told her I would stay with the twins so she could have a break. She questioned me several times, "Are you sure you want to stay here?" "Are you going to be okay here with the twins by yourself?" "Sure, Mom. I can handle it."

So, she left to stay with her friend. I got the twins in bed at around 9 p.m. At about 10 p.m., Donnie got up because he had wet himself and was standing in their bedroom doorway. So, I tried to walk him to the bathroom. I say "try" because to get Donnie from point A to point B was more about patience than progress. "Right here, no. Donnie. Donnie. Donnie. Here. Right here." That went on for a while.

Mind you, the bathroom was all of ten feet from their bedroom. Not a long distance, but it seemed an eternity in time when trying to get him there. So, I took off his clothes, cleaned him up, and dressed him in clean clothes. I had him stand next to his bed while I changed the sheets. That was all going on with Davy asleep in the bed next to Donnie's.

Then, about the time I was finishing with Donnie, about midnight, Davy woke up with a similar but even worse mess. So, I helped Davy through the same basic cleanup procedure that I had just finished with Donnie. The next thing I knew, after a few more go-rounds of the twins getting up and wandering around, it was 5 a.m. and time to get the next day started.

You might wonder why the twins didn't use some kind of absorbent under-wear. Right or wrong, my parents were against diapering them. They viewed using diapers as going backward in the twins' development as people. My mom paid the price for that decision every night. That was my first awareness of a strategy that didn't work as intended. The decision, though well-intended, didn't make things easier for anyone.

Five boys also eat a lot. My dad was the one who did the grocery shopping. Every time he went, he figured out the exact cost of his grocery store items. He totaled all of this in his head so he wouldn't have to stand at the check-out counter using food stamps any longer than absolutely necessary. He never acted embarrassed, but I know he was. My dad was grateful for charity but hated it when he was the recipient.

One Christmas, our church had a "White Gift Service." Several families in the church would wrap canned goods in white tissue paper and donate them to the church. Then, they put the carefully wrapped food items underneath the Christmas tree in the back of the church's sanctuary. The "White Gift Service" was when the church dedicated the food to a needy family in our community. That year they brought the box to our house.

At around age eleven, we didn't attend Sunday morning service for the first time in memory. Our only car sat in the driveway where the tow truck left it the previous night. My mom was coming home from her part-time job and slid off the icy road. She was okay, banged up a little, but now we couldn't drive the only car we had ever again. My parents had basic car insurance, but they couldn't afford "full coverage." So, the insurance we had didn't pay anything toward another car, and we certainly couldn't afford one. We struggled with what we were going to do for transportation. So, we "stayed home from church" (as we called it) that Sunday morning.

Then, that Sunday afternoon, after the church service had finished, I heard something going on outside. So, I peeked from behind our living room curtains and saw two deacons from our church. My dad went to the front door and talked to them for a few minutes. That was a pretty big event for us since we rarely got a visitor, so we were all huddling just a few feet behind Dad in the living room. When they left, my dad turned around and showed us a set of car keys. They belonged to a 1973 Chevy Impala car with a white vinyl roof. My dad said, "The church just gave us a car."

He had a look on his face of shock and disbelief at what had just happened. We couldn't believe it either. Normally we would be running around and jumping and screaming like we just hit the lottery. But this was so huge that our minds couldn't take it in. We were more stunned than excited.

My dad told us that in the church service that morning, the church voted and paid for a used car for our family from a local lot.

Later, I imagined how this gift of a car to the Halcombe family came about. I could see the people and hear their words because, even as a kid, I knew the kind of people they were. After all, I'd spent time with them at church two or three times every week. The people in that church loved us. I knew it, and I could feel it every time I was with them. Their consistent care for us certainly influenced my call to ministry, even though it took years for me to connect the dots.

As I pointed out at the beginning of the chapter, when the center of your personal purpose increases, you also gain skills to better live in your personal domains outside of that circle. In this case, the two domains were "faith" (your church or faith community) and "community" (the place where you live).

Our church even started a special class for the twins. That allowed my dad to sing in the choir and teach Sunday School. My mom also taught, and her space was a Wednesday night missions class for girls. She loved teaching that class and did it for years. Although she had five boys at home, she still wanted to contribute to the ministry at church. So did my dad. At one point, Dad directed our church's Sunday night discipleship program.

At church, life almost seemed normal at times. But not at home. My dad used to say, "I welcome anybody to spend twenty-four hours in this house. It will change their life." I knew he was right.

Just getting the seven of us out the door to go anywhere was a major accomplishment. One time we were ready to leave when we noticed the twins weren't with us as we were walking out the door. We heard them and then found them in the basement with red all over them. Somehow, they found a red spray paint can and shot the paint all over each other. Not only were their clothes ruined, but we also had to go through another round of getting them dressed to get ready to leave the house. Throughout my years of growing up, it seemed like whatever we tried to do was harder, cost more, and took more time than it should.

It never did get any easier for my parents. The minds of the twins never did develop, although their bodies did. As the years wore on, just try to imagine what it was like parenting twin two-year-olds who were the size of grown men.

Things did get better for me because I left home at age eighteen to go to college in Kentucky. Berea College is still one of the only "work your way through" colleges in the country. It allowed me an opportunity to earn a degree.

I didn't even know if I could make it through college since nobody in my family had ever gone. But a pastor of ours in my high school years said in a Sunday night sermon, "College isn't brains. It's work." I thought, "I know how to work." I've since discovered the same is true of leadership. Leadership isn't brains; it's work. So, if you're willing to work, including working on yourself, you can be a great leader.

It was during those college years that I was willing to admit that I believed God wanted me to go into ministry, which I then understood as becoming a pastor of a local church.

I thought I knew what pastors did since I went to church a lot. Plus, I knew a lot about the Bible. So, I figured my Bible knowledge and church experience, along with my growing-up years at home, would prepare me to effectively pastor a church.

I was wrong.

What does this have to do with my personal strategy? It means when I became a pastor, I wrongly believed I had all the strategy I needed because of the difficulty I had growing up and my experience attending church regularly. As it turns out, trusting God through immense challenges and knowing a lot about the Bible are not enough to effectively lead or pastor a church. Effective leadership includes acquiring godly character, but you also must acquire skills in leading an organization to thrive.

*While personal development does precede organizational development, you still must develop the organization.*

# Why Personal Strategy Comes Before Organizational Strategy

Ever notice that organizations, the church included, begin to look like the senior leader over a period of years? Wonder why? All organizations (including churches) mimic the personal character qualities of the key leader because all the decisions that affect the organization come from that leader. His or her initiatives, decisions, and passions show up at the company/church/nonprofit level. Every leader filters the organization's decisions and actions through themselves.

For example, the more fiscally responsible the leader is, the more financially astute the organization is. Likewise, risk-averse leaders won't move the organization forward because they themselves won't move forward. A church led by a pastor afraid to try new things won't try new things. They will meet, discuss, and hash and rehash the idea, but they won't move it forward when the leader keeps the brakes on.

Evangelistic pastors lead evangelistic churches. Prayer-focused leaders lead the church to be the "house of prayer" God commanded it to be. On the other hand, pastors who possess a clear personal purpose (and a clear organizational purpose, as we'll discuss later) lead balanced, effective congregations.

So, your Personal Strategy centers on your personal purpose. It shows the primary necessity of personal development. If you don't develop personally, you won't accomplish all God wants to do through you. The example of Jesus shows us this. But also note that Jesus did not only work out His personal development. He created an organizational strategy to fulfill His personal purpose. That organizational strategy was (and is) the church.

## The Organizational Strategy

*You need an organization to effect change beyond yourself.*

Jesus's mission began with His personal development (the Personal Strategy), but it necessarily included more because He wanted His impact to extend beyond Himself.

The same is true of you.

If you want to effect change beyond yourself, you need to include an organization. A businessperson needs a business. An entrepreneur uses a for-profit or nonprofit corporation. A stay-at-home parent requires a family.

For you, your personal development is primary, but it is not solitary. If you only develop yourself, then only you are impacted. *If you want your impact to extend beyond you, you need a mechanism beyond you, an organization.* This also holds true for the church. It's incumbent on the leader to develop personally. But if that church leader does not develop the church organizationally, that leader truncates their impact. Unfortunately, when church leaders don't develop the church organizationally, the effectiveness of that church is also severely limited.

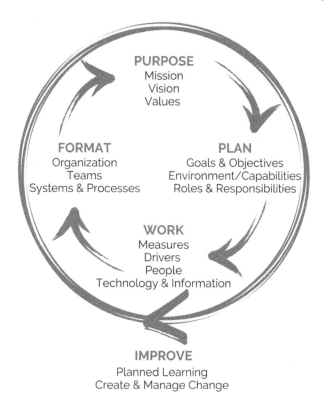

Jesus developed a new organization because His personal mission required it. *(Chapter 11 discusses in-depth how Jesus used organizational strategy.)*

The Organizational Strategy outlines how Jesus launched His organization, the church. It shows the categories of work that churches need to do to accomplish their mission.

→ **Purpose.** This includes mission (why your church exists), vision (how your church will look in three or five years [maybe ten years, you choose] when the mission goes well), and your core values.

→ **Plan.** Your written accountable plan to achieve the organization's goals/ objectives. One person is responsible for each objective, and each objective contains a deadline for completion.

→ **Work.** The tasks you and your team must perform to fulfill your plan. People must work the processes, include a way to measure the progress, and manage technology and information.

→ **Format.** The structure (organization, teams, systems, and processes) your church/organization needs to accomplish the work, the plan, and the mission.

→ **Improve.** To continue to progress, your church/organization must regularly evaluate her current state in light of what you believe God wants you to achieve. As your church continually adapts to new input, your understanding and implementation of change management will determine, to a very high degree, your level of success. To do it the way Jesus did it, you have to also include reward and recognition.

*Jesus used strategy to build the church. We do well to follow.*

There are a few things to keep in mind. Since we live in a different age, the components (technology, for example) under each heading may change somewhat, but the overall design stays the same. Another thing to consider is the level of complexity of each major heading differs according to the size (mainly) of the organization. Yet, even with some variation, every church or organization, if it is to progress, needs these five major components. Even if you are the only person in the organization, you need these five building blocks in mind as you move forward.

Jesus lays out His organizational strategy in the sixteenth chapter of the gospel of Matthew. In Matthew 16:18, we find the first mention in the New Testament of this new organization, the "church." This word "church" (and the concept) comes from the lips of Jesus. He says it after He clarifies His personal purpose with His key leaders. (A key takeaway here: Even the Son of God included His key leaders in the discovery of the church's purpose. Jesus did not craft it alone and then share it. He developed it with His key players. Churches benefit most when they do the same.) Once His and the organization's purpose is clear, Jesus then lays out the plan, the work, and the format and initiates the improvement process. Jesus used all five of these elements, and so should we if we want to build the church as Jesus did.

A pastor told me yesterday, "We (our church) just go from week to week." That alone tells you the church does not do well. They struggle to even maintain their current level of ministry. I know they don't possess a clear mission, and they don't have a written plan. Unsure of the work with a fuzzy format, not much happens. Gratefully, that pastor wants to learn the strategy of Jesus so they can improve their impact with the gospel. He understands it takes more than biblical preaching to build a great church.

The good news is any church leader can improve. All great leaders *continually* improve. That's one of the hallmarks of leaders God uses. We become better leaders, and our churches become better churches when we improve our strategy based on how Jesus did it. To lead organizations that change the world, we must not just say what Jesus said. We have to do what Jesus did. What did Jesus do? Jesus led organizationally.

Here's the outline of how it can look in your life. The leadership strategy of Jesus incorporates all areas of your life (personal and organizational) and gives you a rhythm to ensure nothing gets missed.

*Chapter 2*

# WHY DON'T LEADERS MENTION STRATEGY MORE OFTEN?

I f it's true that great leaders regularly use strategy, why don't they mention it more often? For example, I heard another podcast yesterday from a great leader. He started and grew a very effective church. Then he led a major initiative for one of our country's largest churches. The major initiative also does extremely well. So, in the interview, how do you think he explained the growth of the church he started and now the incredible success of this major initiative?

"Remember, it's Jesus Who builds the church. You don't do it. I don't do it. Jesus does it." Sound familiar? Conference speakers, seminars, and podcasts often say similar things.

But is that really the whole story?

If Jesus is the One who built this leader's church (and subsequent ministry), why doesn't Jesus build everybody's church? Is Jesus picking winners? I posed this question at the beginning of the book.

The truth is that this effective leader used strategy (which absolutely includes relying on God) that contributed to that church's success. I know this because I know that leader personally and watched the church develop. But why didn't he say so?

In my associations with effective leaders, they typically don't mention strategy for the following reasons. (There may be more reasons than these two, but these seem to be pretty consistent.)

## Humility

That leader who said, "It's Jesus Who builds the church" (and so many others in conferences and podcasts the world over) probably gave all the credit to Jesus because he is humble. He realizes God does things only God can do. But leaders also say, "Only Jesus does it" because they cannot imagine *not* doing the things that they did to make those ministries effective.

But those "other things" are the difference makers when it comes to leading ministry.

When I first came to Columbus, the network I directed had a committee whose job was to help start new churches. At the time, they hadn't started a church in the previous five years. There were two "church plants" they had helped before the five-year dry spell. One of those new churches was surviving with about seventy people or so. It was deemed a success. The other church plant never did get traction. They only had a handful of people attending in one of the fastest-growing counties in the United States. The little money those attendees gave to the church was given away to hurting people. They disbanded shortly after that. So, we met as a committee to evaluate what was happening.

In talking to the committee, I asked, "What's the difference between those two churches? Why did one succeed and the other fail?" One of the committee members gave the all-too-common answer, "Well, the difference was God, right?" I said, "No. I have been to both those church plants, and God was there at both of them."

Furthermore, theologically, we know God is everywhere. The difference between success and failure was not God. He did not (and does not, as far as I can tell) orchestrate churches to fail. The reason churches fail is because of what they do or don't do.

Consider the first church I pastored after graduating from seminary. Years before my arrival, they sold part of the plot of land they owned. This sale left them with eight-tenths (0.8) of an acre of total land. Additionally, they tore down an old building on that property to build a newer building.

These two decisions (to sell part of their property and to build a smaller building) formed their strategy. It was a bad strategy. They made two fatal mistakes. The first strategic error was selling property that leaves you only eight-tenths of an acre. Their thirty-nine parking spaces and building maxed out the entire .8 of an acre.

From a strategic perspective, the second catastrophic move was to tear down a larger building to build a smaller building. What that church actually did was prevent new people from attending. To make matters worse, they did not have enough room for the people already attending. Unfortunately, many churches make bad strategic moves, even though their intentions are good. In this case, like many others, no matter what they thought they were doing, their bad strategy set in motion years of decline. They never recovered.

Did Jesus tear down the building and sell part of the property? No, He didn't. The people did. They made those unfortunate errors. So, even when a leader says, "Only Jesus builds the church," their humility may prevent them from seeing they actually have a lot to do with how well things go.

Humility does prevent leaders from admitting the part they play in growing a church, but it's not the only reason leaders don't include strategy when they tell how their ministry has grown. Some leaders innately think strategically.

## Natural Gifting

When world-class leaders "give all the credit to Jesus," I don't think they intentionally mislead people. I believe they are gifted in strategic thinking, so they never imagine other leaders don't think that way.

When my son was in first grade, he wanted to play tee-ball. His team needed a coach, and I got recruited even though I know little about baseball. I attended many coaching clinics to learn how to coach a tee-ball team. A seasoned pro led an incredible batting/hitting clinic. That leader broke down the motion of hitting a baseball into seven different steps. For each one of those steps, he placed a baseball card on different parts of the body to show the visual cues of where to look, how to position your feet, when and how to turn your body, and how to level a swing to connect with the ball. It was amazing.

In the course of the clinic, he mentioned that often the worst coaches are natural hitters. Naturally gifted athletes did not have to figure out how to connect the bat to the ball. They just hit it. If you were to ask a natural hitter how to hit the ball, he would say, "Walk up to the baseball (home plate) and do this." Then, he would hit the ball out of the park. The motions of hitting come so naturally to him that he either doesn't know the steps he takes or he doesn't know how to explain them.

World-class leaders are a lot like world-class athletes. Naturally gifted leaders just know the right moves to make. They often cannot explain how they know. They just intuit it because of how they grew up and how their minds work.

The problem comes with leaders who didn't grow up in a well-led church. That's where I was. My background did not include examples of great leaders. Maybe yours didn't either. But I did learn, and so can you.

Great leaders don't talk a lot about "how-to" from the pulpits and podcasts because they cannot imagine someone leading anything, especially a church, if they aren't operating strategically. Great leaders don't mention the "how-tos" or the thinking behind "Jesus builds the church" because they think all leaders already know to:

→ Possess a clear mission all your leaders know and use.
→ Make sure the church's lawn is mown and landscaped.
→ Confront a problem when first discovered (after figuring out the best approach).
→ Invest ten to fifteen hours each week preparing a biblical, clear, relevant, and interesting message.
→ Make financially contributing to the church a requirement for all your key leaders and check (or have someone else check) to ensure they are giving.
→ Strategize frequently on how to increase attendance, evangelism, discipleship, prayer, and baptisms. I say "frequently," but it's really a constant. Strategic leaders constantly evaluate everything that's happening to improve it. In this instance, "constantly" is not hyperbole.
→ Regularly assess your leaders' effectiveness and make necessary adjustments.
→ Retool/restructure your leaders and the organization for greater effectiveness.
→ Remove, retrain, or transfer ineffective leaders (this includes volunteers and paid staff).

→ Manage the budget so your spending does not exceed the budgeted amount.

→ Make sure nobody else spends more than the budget.

→ Create new initiatives to increase the impact of your mission.

→ Meet with your leaders at least once a month.

→ Develop a leadership development process to constantly train and raise up new leaders.

→ Develop expectations for leaders and hold them accountable to fulfill them.

→ Refuse to pursue ministries or initiatives that don't fit your mission or culture

For great leaders, this list falls into the category of no-brainers. It's just a representative list. Effective leaders don't function without them. But many of us don't know these things. We hear "just leave it up to God," and we leave it up to God. Then, we wonder why the church doesn't do well when we make bad decisions organizationally.

So, you see some leaders grow up with leadership. They cannot imagine a life without it. Plus, they certainly wouldn't avoid these fundamental leadership principles to just "wait on the Lord." They know how to lead because they saw it, lived it, breathed it, and practiced leading.

The problem for me was my life wasn't like that. Maybe yours wasn't either.

Growing up in a rural area, I knew some leaders. I had football coaches and a high school principal. But I lived mostly among non-leaders, in the church anyway. They were wonderful, godly people. But they didn't lead. I didn't see great examples of leadership at church. I honestly don't think many (if any) of them led other people in their day jobs. In the shoptalk of the day, it was a big deal for a person to "be over people" in any vein of life. Few could imagine it. Most didn't want it.

In that world, reality looked more like this:

→ If the church's lawn has not been mown, it's because the mower is broken or the guy mowing it didn't show up. That made it okay to leave the grass uncut, even for a Sunday morning service.

→ When a problem arises, you hope (and pray) it will go away because you don't "feel right" telling somebody else what to do, especially in church. You think God should lead them to the right answer, and it would be wrong for you to "play God" and confront them. You also don't deal with the problem because it would cause you a lot of internal anxiety. Furthermore, you won't risk the relationship even when you know the person is doing wrong. A leader who didn't handle conflict well told me, "I mainly want people to like seeing me at the local grocery store." When people avoid conflict because it will make them (or others) uncomfortable, they forfeit their opportunity to make a positive impact.

→ Sermon preparation would be great if you had time to do it. But because you need to visit the hospitals, answer phone calls, and do "what the people paying your salary expect you to do," rarely does the time become available. "What's expected" could mean anything from repairing plumbing for church members (true story) or taking somebody to their doctor's appointment (also true story). When I heard about all he did, I asked one bi-vocational pastor, "When do you find time to prepare for your sermons?" He said, "You want me to tell you the truth?" "Yes." "I get up on Sunday morning and start reading (the Bible). When I get an idea, that's what I preach." You can probably guess that the pastor left the ministry, and the church continues to struggle.

→ Financially, you hope people give, but you are dead set against ever checking (or having someone else check) the personal giving records of people before you put them into leadership. I'm still not sure why. The typical answer I hear about why pastors don't find out what people are giving (or have someone who keeps the records let them know, in frame worked amounts) is: "I wouldn't trust myself to not treat people differently if I knew what amount of money they gave to the church." The pastor is saying that the reason you don't check what people actually give is the pastor's personal issue.

→ You preach and ask people to invite others and share the gospel and then get disappointed when they don't. So, you preach and ask again, or in a different way. You call it a different name or think if you keep talking about it, people will eventually "get it" or start doing it. Instead of launching a new initiative or style of worship or recruiting new leaders who share the gospel, you keep doing the same things and expecting different results. It doesn't work.

See the difference? Effective leaders create what needs to happen. They clearly see where God wants the church to go and make adjustments, launch initiatives, hire new staff, rearrange the org chart, or any number of things to move the church to grow and reach people. *In other words, as I mentioned in the opening, effective leaders develop and implement a strategy to get the results they believe God wants.*

This all may sound disheartening to you. I hope it doesn't. You should not be discouraged because you can learn and apply all you need to grow a ministry that impacts the world positively.

***You can learn to lead effectively. You can improve your strategy.***

All leadership skills are learnable. I didn't grow up seeing strategic leaders, but I learned how to lead. This book was written to share those same concepts with you. You can learn to make major kingdom impact even if you didn't grow up learning how. *The Leadership Strategy of Jesus* isn't just a list of leadership skills (although many are included). It's a process that puts all those skills into the framework Jesus used to create the largest organization on the planet. You can (and should) use this same system of leading if you want kingdom results.

*Chapter 3*

# MINISTRY MYTHS ABOUT STRATEGY

When I pastored a local church, we regularly had people from church to our house for dinner. Some of the people who came to our home were church members, while others were people who had recently started attending our church. On one of those occasions, one of our guests (who was relatively new at the church) saw Michael Hammer's book *Beyond Reengineering* on my bookshelf. He asked, "Why are you reading that?" I answered, "It shows me how to plan and lead better in the church." He replied, "I think you should only use the Bible to lead in the church." I don't know why he thought I shouldn't improve my leadership skills, especially when I wanted to do a great job leading an area in the church that involved over three thousand people. I do know he and his family quit attending the church.

## Sacred and Secular Divide?

Like so many others, our guest thought there was some artificial divide in our lives between the secular (stuff outside the church) and sacred (stuff inside the church). The crazy thing? Those same people would argue we should be the same at our workplaces as we are in church. Many sermons tell us we need to be the same on Monday as we are on Sunday. If that's true, we should also be the same on Sunday as we are on Monday. That principle also goes for strategy.

After all, if it isn't morally wrong to strategize at work on Monday, then how can it be morally wrong to strategize for church on Sunday? To take it a step further, if it is morally wrong to strategize at church, then it is morally wrong to strategize at work, and Christians should not work at companies that use strategy. So, if you really believe churches should not strategize, then you should not take a paycheck from a business that does.

Of course, this off-kilter thinking does not come from the Bible. Unfortunately, this isn't the only Ministry Myth when it comes to strategy.

## Questions About Using Strategy in the Church

Here are some questions for those who believe we should not use "secular" or "business" learning or principles (or whatever moniker they use) at church:

→ If the sinless Son of God thought it necessary (He didn't do anything unintentionally) to use strategy and leadership principles (that businesses also use), why do we think it's wrong?

→ If using "business principles" (which are really God's principles) is wrong inside the church, would it not also be wrong to use business principles outside the church? After all, if it's wrong, it's wrong. For example, lying is wrong whether you are at church, at home, or at work. It's the same with all other sins. If you are saying using business principles at church is wrong, you must also admit people are sinning by using these same principles even when they are at work.

→ What exactly do you mean when you say, "You shouldn't bring 'business' into the church"? Most churches regularly use many of the same tools that businesses use: pens, markers, paper, computers, printers, and software, for example. Is it wrong to use these tools? None of these tools started as "church tools." They all started with businesses. Businesses convert pulp into paper, manufacture pens and markers, and build computers, printers, and software. If it's okay to use these tools, why would it not be okay to use the principles businesses use to build these tools we use most every day?

When it comes to the use of buildings for churches to use, churches also follow "business" principles in building these buildings. Churches use foundations, walls, headers, studs, sheetrock, and building codes in their buildings. Is this somehow wrong? Aren't these also "business" principles? At the very least, churches use principles of design and construction. By the way, nowhere does the Bible say we should use buildings. Does that make it wrong somehow?

## The Last (Most Important) Question

If it is wrong to use "business" in the church, where does the Bible say it is wrong? If you agree (and some may not) that the Bible shows us what is right and wrong, then the Bible would tell us if something is wrong.

This author's baseline orientation toward right and wrong is the Bible. If the Bible says it's wrong, then it's wrong. If the Bible does *not* tell us it is wrong (either by command or by principle), then it is not wrong. Furthermore, if the Bible does not say it is wrong, then it is okay for a believer to do it. (You might have to let that one sink in a little bit.)

I've read and taught the Bible in church for many years. I also taught classes at a Bible college and master's level students at a seminary for seven years. I can tell you the Bible says nothing about using an organizational chart or a Venn diagram or computer software. Since the Bible does not say using charts, diagrams, and software is wrong, then it is acceptable (and not a sin) for churches to use them. This does not mean churches *have* to use them. But it does mean churches are allowed by God to use them.

This flows against the pastor who says, "It's all Jesus." It's really not all Jesus—contextually. If it were all Jesus, we would not need pastors, chairs, air conditioning, or buildings. I wonder if we sometimes say "It's all Jesus" to absolve ourselves of the responsibility of figuring out how to run an organization?

Furthermore, although many church leaders think strategy is not necessary or somehow "unspiritual," Jesus did not see it that way. Jesus used strategy as a means to accomplish His purpose on the planet. He used strategy and expects us to use strategy because strategy works to accomplish major undertakings. What's more, Jesus's leadership strategy shows up in churches, nonprofits, and for-profit corporations the world over, even if they don't know Jesus used it.

This book's perspective is that we should not just say what Jesus said. We should do what Jesus did. And what Jesus did was to launch the largest organization in the history of the world: the church. His launching undeniably included strategy.

But this book does not create a *new* strategy. It uncovers the very strategy Jesus used for worldwide and eternal impact.

Here's the good news: You and I can use the same strategy to increase our impact both in our personal lives and in the organizations we lead. I have done that and am doing that. The many leaders and churches I coach use it, and they use it to increase their effectiveness to accomplish their mission.

My hope and prayer are that you will operate more strategically when you see how Jesus did it. It's helped many leaders get over the false idea that strategy is somehow wrong or unspiritual. "Using strategy brings the world into the church" is a great ploy of the devil, but it's only one scheme. If the devil can make leaders believe using strategy is somehow wrong, he limits their effectiveness and potential. That thinking relegates leaders to mediocre results. Here are other examples of wrongheaded thinking that limit our effectiveness. Check out these Ministry Myths and see if you have been influenced by any of them.

## Myth #1: "We Don't Plan; We Just Pray."

### George Müller Just Prayed, and the Miraculous Happened

A famous example people use to promote the "We don't plan; we just pray" Ministry Myth comes from George Müller. (George Müller [1805–1898] was a well-known preacher best remembered for starting and directing a large orphanage in England.)

"One of the best-loved Müller stories comes to us from Abigail Townsend Luffe. When she was a child, her father assisted Müller, and she spent time at Ashley Down. Early one morning, Müller led her into the long dining room set for breakfast but without food, praying, 'Dear Father, we thank Thee for what Thou art going to give us to eat.' There was a knock at the door; it was the baker, unable to sleep because he was sure the Lord wanted him to bake bread for Müller. 'Children,' Müller said, 'We not only have bread but fresh bread.' Almost immediately, they heard a second knock. It was the milkman; the milk cart had broken down outside the orphanage, and he offered the milk to the children, completing their meal."[3]

## What We Miss About George Müller

Here (and throughout Müller's autobiography)[4] we see God provided incredibly for George Müller's orphans. But God did not answer his prayers in a vacuum. It wasn't that George Müller just prayed this prayer without a context. From Müller's own words, God provided as George developed and worked a strategy to house, feed, and care for the orphans. George Müller definitely prayed. But prayer was part of his strategy and not the only part of his strategy.

## George Müller Clarified the Purpose

George Müller first started by developing the purpose for his orphanage. His June 12, 1833, diary notes: "This morning, I felt that we should do something for the poor. We have given bread to them daily for some time now. I longed to establish a school for the boys and girls, read Scriptures to them, and speak to them about the Lord."[5] George wanted to feed the orphans, and he determined establishing a school was a good way to accomplish it. We see that George "felt" he should do something, and then he went and did it.

## Müller Developed the Plan

On February 21, 1834: "I began to form a plan to establish an institution for the spread of the gospel at home and abroad. I trust this matter is of God."[6]

On February 25, 1834: "I was led again to pray about forming a new missionary institution and felt more certain that we should do so."[7]

Then, on March 5, 1834, his autobiography states: "This evening at a public meeting, brother Craik and I stated the principles on which we intend to establish our institution for the spread of the gospel at home and abroad. There was nothing outwardly impressive in the number of people present or in our speeches. May the Lord graciously grant His blessing upon the institution which will be called 'The Scriptural Knowledge Institution for Home and Abroad.'"[8]

After listing seven principles, George writes "The Goals of the Institution." He started with three. George's planning in no way undercuts George's praying. It just shows us that God answers prayers of faith when accompanied by a thorough strategy.

### Back to the Fresh Bread and Milk Cart Story

If George had not clarified the purpose of the orphanage and developed the plan for the orphanage, he would not have needed any milk and bread. Without orphans, there's no need for food to feed them. George Müller trusted God to build an orphanage and then depended upon God to provide. He followed the same strategy Jesus followed to see God do the miraculous. It's the same strategy effective churches use today.

So, why did George record all this? Why didn't he just do what God led him to do? H. Wayland Lincoln tells us in the Conclusion of George Müller's autobiography:[9]

> "What God has done for Mr. Müller and his associates, we cannot doubt that, under the same conditions, He will do for every believing disciple of Christ. Not only did Mr. Müller trust in God that all the financial means he needed would be furnished, but that, in answer to prayer, wisdom would be given him to manage the work. The result surpassed his highest expectations. If anyone will undertake any Christian work in a similar spirit and on the same principles, his labor will meet with a similar result."

God used George Müller to provide for over 10,000 orphans.[10] He traveled over 200,000 miles (in the 1800s) and preached to 3,000,000 people.

What's the takeaway from George Müller's life?

You can do it, too.

How? You have to pray, definitely. But don't rely only on praying. Go ahead and do what you feel you should do to further Christ's kingdom. It's how all (from my experience) great endeavors begin. You must clarify the purpose for what you're doing, develop the plan, do the work, format as needed (Mr. Müller's purpose required the building of orphanages), and consistently evaluate and improve the plan and all that follows.

*Then, you, too, will experience what only God can do.*

## Myth #2: "It's All God. It Has Nothing to Do with Us."

It may be intended as hyperbole. But as stated, it's dead wrong.

How could the statement "It's all God, and it has nothing to do with us" be wrong? It's wrong because it excludes a key piece of God's creation: human beings. The truth is God includes us. Why else would He create us? Does it make any biblical sense for God to create humankind and then leave them totally out of the picture when it comes to what God wants to accomplish? From the first chapter of Genesis, when He created human beings, His plan decidedly and directly used us. It still does.

As we peruse the pages of Scripture, we see a consistent pattern. God's work necessarily involves people. He used Moses to free His people from the Egyptians (Exodus 3:1–10). God called Abram to "be a blessing to other nations" (Genesis 12). The Lord God sent His Son through Mary (Luke 1:26–38). This pattern of God using women and men continues throughout the New Testament. Jesus's final words to His followers punctuate not just the involvement of people but our responsibility to carry out God's plan. Often called the "Great Commission," Matthew makes it clear God uses people: "Go, therefore, and make disciples of all nations, baptizing them in the name of the Father and of the Son and of the Holy Spirit, teaching them to observe everything I have commanded you. And remember, I am with you always, to the end of the age" (Matthew 28:19–20, CSB). Who did Jesus intend to do the going? People. You and me.

God's plan started with God, to be sure. But He chose (and chooses) us to fulfill it. The Bible pushes the point further in the "Roll Call of Faith" in Hebrews 11:

"And what more can I say? Time is too short for me to tell about Gideon, Barak, Samson, Jephthah, David, Samuel, and the prophets, who by faith conquered kingdoms, administered justice, obtained promises, shut the mouths of lions, quenched the raging of fire, escaped the edge of the sword, gained strength in weakness, became mighty in battle, and put foreign armies to flight. Women received their dead, raised to life again. Other people were tortured, not accepting release, so that they might gain a better resurrection. Others experienced mockings and scourgings as well as bonds and imprisonment. They were stoned, they were sawed in two, they died by the sword, they wandered about in sheepskins, in goatskins, destitute, afflicted, and mistreated. The world was not worthy of them. They wandered in deserts and on mountains, hiding in caves and holes in the ground" (Hebrews 11:32–38, CSB).

What stands out in this passage is that this is a listing of *people*. This chapter shows that human beings, called and empowered by God, did the work. Notice this passage does not say, "God did it alone." The writer of Hebrews names others. Biblically, you cannot support the idea that God's work excludes people.

If someone told you, "It's all God. It has nothing to do with you," you may have misunderstood what that leader really meant. I'm hoping you don't fall for this Ministry Myth. God wants to include you.

"Lord, what are human beings that you care for them, mere mortals that you think of them?" (Psalm 144:3).

## Myth #3: "The Bible Does Not Tell Us to Use Strategy"

Here's another common misunderstanding: "Well, if the Bible does not say we should use it, then we should not use it." The backdrop for this Ministry Myth is a faulty hermeneutic. (A hermeneutic is a principle for interpreting the Bible.) Saying "if the Bible does not tell us to do it, then we should not do it" can sound somewhat spiritual on the surface. But once we apply it to other areas, we see why this myth is a fable. This thinking misunderstands how we apply the Bible to life. The truth is, we don't have to have a direct biblical command for everything we do. As a matter of fact, the Bible does not even address most of life's activities.

Let's look at a few examples:

- → The Bible does not say we should use buildings.
- → The Bible never tells me to use electricity.
- → The Bible does not promote riding in internal combustion or electric vehicles (automobiles).
- → The Bible does not direct the use of ink pens.

You see where this is going.

Here are a few more things the Bible does not specifically endorse:

→ Telephones
→ The postal system
→ Email
→ Scripture via an electronic device
→ Lawnmowers

Do you know what's striking about this list? Most churches use everything I just listed. Churches and church people regularly walk into church buildings, turn on the lights, ride in cars, write with pens, pick up the phone to make a call, mail stuff (though less than in previous years), email friends, look up Bible verses on their computer, tablet or phone, and mow (or have someone else mow) the church's lawn (as well as their lawns at home).

Is using any of these things "bringing the world into the church"?

No.

Even though the Bible does not expressly tell us to use a phone or the like, it's okay to use one. God grants us the freedom to use things that make our lives better, even if the Bible does not directly tell us to do them.

Instead of thinking, *I cannot do it unless the Bible tells me to do it*, it's better to realize we are free to do anything the Bible does not prohibit, either through a direct command or a biblical principle. That freedom means we can use strategy.

## Myth #4: "Churches Should Not Use Business Strategy"

The problem with this myth is attribution. People call it "business strategy." In reality, businesses did not create business strategy. God did that. He is the One Who created people to function in predictable ways, whether those people work in a business or a church or a nonprofit organization. Leaders who use strategy recognize this reality and implement it because they want their organization to effectively accomplish the reason they exist. So, strategies are not really "business strategies" per se. They are strategies God created that businesses happen to use because they want to succeed and make money. Since we have a higher calling, why would we not use what God created to reach people? Let's give credit where credit is due.

## How God Used Strategy in the Sending of His Son

After all, God Himself used strategy. Let's take a look at just one example.

Why did God wait four hundred years between the Old and New Testaments before sending Jesus to the earth? Through His prophets in the Old Testament, God repeatedly promised a Messiah. Over and over again, from the "first gospel" in Genesis 3:15, throughout the Torah and then through the Prophets, God told people a Redeemer is coming. That being the case, why would He take so long? Why the huge gap of time between the Old Testament and the New? Many Bible students believe these four hundred "years of silence" readied the world to receive the gospel. Here are a couple of strategic reasons why God may have waited those four hundred years.

**Pax Romana.** Rome dominated the world at the time of Christ. But it hadn't always been that way. The Pax Romana ("peace of Rome") developed during the intertestamental period ("between the testaments," meaning between the Old Testament and the New Testament). The control of the Roman Empire, even with its vast excesses, brought a new era of safety to the land. This "peace of Rome" paved the way for missionaries to travel and spread the good news of Christ without being bushwhacked by bandits along the way. Before the peace of Rome, numerous warring factions regularly waylaid travelers. Strategically, the times between the testaments created an environment for the gospel to transmit more easily via roadways and waterways by the time Jesus arrived.

**Hellenization.** The word "Hellenization" derives from *Hellas*, which is the Greek word for Greece. Between the two testaments, the world "Greeked." Greek culture and influence grew. Hellenization, this spread of the Greek culture, necessarily included how people communicated with each other. The Greek language became the lingua franca of the world at that time, largely due to the conquests of Alexander the Great. The first people to put the Hebrew Old Testament into a different language chose Greek to be the Bible's first translation (called the LXX, or Septuagint).

This global use of Greek in the first century is often compared to English in this century. Imagine how much easier Christianity spread at that time because people spoke the same language! Conversely, it's hard to fathom the difficulty in spreading the good news if you had to communicate that news in umpteen different languages. Every day run-of-the-mill people used this "koine" (meaning "common") Greek to buy and sell goods and to communicate on the first-century streets. This use of the Greek language developed during the time between the Old and New Testaments. Strategically, God used Greek in the writing of the New Testament. That commonality of language did not exist before the four hundred years between the Old and New Testaments.

So, even the time-between-the-testaments show us God Himself operates strategically. This also tells us strategy is not confined to business. God created and uses strategy. *He doesn't just whammy His will into place. He takes well-considered steps to accomplish His purposes.*

So should we.

## Myth #5: "It's Too Pragmatic"

"It makes too much sense." A pastor told me that as we looked at an additional building to fulfill what we had described as our next initiative.

"It's too pragmatic."

Really?

It is as if it needs to be weird or mysterious or momentous to be spiritual. Leaders miss God's best by camping out in a holy cocoon "waiting for God to do something" when they have not done the work of determining their direction, establishing a plan, doing the work, reformatting the organization, and changing to improve.

Admittedly, some leaders can be too pragmatic if they violate biblical mandates or principles. The pragmatism the strategy of Jesus uses is what the Bible describes as wisdom. It's common sense but within the guardrails of Scripture. Jesus did not (and we should not) be in the "ends justify the means" camp. That Machiavellianism rails against God's will and God's ways. The strategy of Jesus advocates wisdom, but wisdom within biblical parameters.

But it's also important to add that Jesus's strategy does not operate within manmade limitations that appear nowhere in Scripture. One example of a manmade mandate is the type of musical instruments a church chooses. Nowhere does the Bible dictate which instruments to use or which instruments to avoid. In your local context, you get to choose what you use. It may be best for your situation to select particular musical instruments and avoid others. Let's just not pretend the Bible directs those choices.

## "We Don't Know What God Wants Us to Do"

Obviously, God knows what we don't know. It's true that we don't know for sure what to do. But "we don't know what God wants to do" *is a starting point, not a destination.* God appoints leaders to figure it out with His guidance and then to go for it. Paul knew this when he told the believers in Colossae, "For this cause we also, since the day we heard it, do not cease to pray for you, and to desire that ye might be filled with the knowledge of His will in all wisdom and spiritual understanding" (Colossians 1:9, KJV). To be effective, the spiritual must show up in shoe leather. Without a plan, the so-called spiritual "waiting on God" turns out to be just . . . waiting.

Think for a moment about the physical movements of Jesus when He was on the earth. How did He get from one place to the next?

Ready?

He walked.

Every day. Plodded. Jesus physically moved His body to get from Point A to Point B. He did not wait or loiter or thumb twiddle. Furthermore, God the Father did not whisk Jesus's body from one locale to another through a heavenly portal. Jesus's mode of transportation did not consist of an invisible surfboard that buoyed His body above the grime and grit of the dirt paths. No, He walked. Mundane and natural, Jesus put one foot in front of the other to get from one place to another. He did not wait for a message painted in the sky or for the mood to strike. He went forward. So should you. Don't wait for a voice when you have a verse. We sometimes say we "wait on God." Let's just make sure God isn't waiting on us.

*Chapter 4*

# STRATEGIES THAT DON'T WORK

## Failed Strategy #1

*Prayer Isn't Preparation for the Strategy. Prayer is the Strategy.*

A few years ago, I attended a meeting of Christian leaders. They purported to develop a strategy. Each of the attendees led networks of churches like the one I lead. The meeting's organizer gave each of us a big piece of paper to draw on and share our strategies. One leader wrote the word "PRAY" at the top of his page. He then drew arrows down to the bottom of the page where he had drawn churches—little buildings with steeples on the top of each one. When it came his time to present, he said, "Pray. That's all we are supposed to do. Just pray."

It looked a little like this:

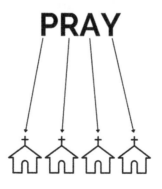

That was it.

That leader believed and promoted this Ministry Myth. The results in his network showed it. That church network experienced years of decline in the number and the participation of churches. They struggled to pay their bills and created no new avenues of ministry or impact. He retired a few years later.

When it was my turn, I shared our network's beginning strategy with the room. The strategy that helped us add churches each year and continually increase revenue, involvement, and impact. It was the strategy Jesus used. Just as I wound down my talk, a voice from the back of the room shouted, "What about prayer?" I responded that we need to pray (and I pray every day), but we need to do more than pray.

Don't make the mistake of thinking the strategy of Jesus downplays prayer. Prayer plays a key role, but it doesn't form the whole strategy. This author prays every day, usually once in the morning, throughout the day, and then my wife and I pray each night. This is in addition to keeping a spiritual journal most days and fasting one day a month for the last several years. Prayer must be daily and vital, but it is not total. You absolutely must pray, but you definitely need to do more than pray.

That shout from the back of the room agreed with this Ministry Myth: "Prayer isn't preparation for the strategy. Prayer is the strategy." It's not true. Prayer is an important part of the strategy, but it is only a part of the strategy.

How do we know this to be a myth?

***Because Jesus did not operate this way.***

Certainly, Jesus prayed. He prayed every day. Often, He prayed several times a day. But Jesus did more than pray. The sinless Son of God also clarified His and the church's purpose, created a plan, worked the plan, formatted the organization, and developed a system of improvement. If praying were all we needed, then Jesus would only have prayed.

For those who believe "Praying is all we need," I wonder, do they pray all day? Do they pray eight to ten hours a day? If prayer truly were the only answer, then all we should do is pray.

Prayer is definitely a key part of the strategy of Jesus. It's in the "Favor with God" quadrant in the Personal Strategy.

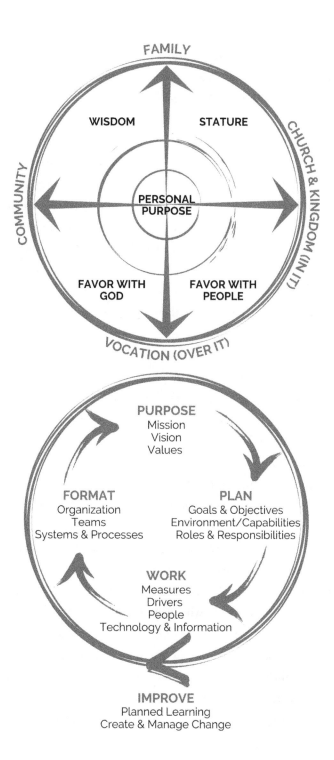

Indeed, we must pray to "increase in favor with God." But as you can see from the strategy of Jesus diagram, much more than prayer is needed to accomplish the purpose Christ entrusted to us effectively.

***Jesus did more than pray. So should we.***

## Failed Strategy #2

*We Need to Disciple People, and They Will Organically Share Their Faith.*

I've clocked over thirty years in full-time ministry. I'm still hearing this. At a recent ordination council meeting, where pastoral candidates are vetted before being ordained, the candidate was asked: "How will you lead the church to do evangelism?" The candidate shared, "I will lead them to become more like Christ, then evangelism will happen organically." His answer revealed his acolyte status. This faulty precept gets way too much repeating. "Once people deepen their faith, they will share the gospel and invite others to church" is a myth for two reasons:

### 1. It does not work.

As I mentioned, I have heard this faulty precept for over thirty years. But in thirty years of full-time ministry, I have never seen it work. It doesn't work in the rural area where I was reared. It doesn't work in the large metro areas where I have served. This way of thinking does not produce results in the inner city, suburbs, or ex-urban communities.

Have you ever seen it work?

What really happens when people get "deeper in the faith"?

"Deeper in the faith," the way churches typically translate it, means people align their lives more completely with the Bible, develop Christlike attributes, and become more like Christ. These are good things. But the unfortunate byproduct of walking more closely with Christ in the way churches typically do is that you grow further away from people who need Christ. As your friendships develop deeper inside the church, your friendships outside the church erode. Dialogue decreases. Facetime drops. Without an intentional effort to share your faith, you quit sharing your life with people who don't attend church with you. The "organic results" of going deeper are isolation and insulation from unbelievers, not evangelism. We need to deep-six the "grow deeper first" Ministry Myth.

The second reason "go deeper and after people go deeper, they will evangelize" doesn't work is:

## 2. Jesus did not get His disciples deeper before they shared their faith.

They went "deeper" and "broader" at the same time. Jesus did not put them in a sequence. He did both. It's a two-pronged parallel strategy.

When I became director of a network of churches, one of the churches I encountered met in a school. The church existed for a few years at that point. It hadn't grown or realized their vision of property yet, but they were hopeful. In talking with the pastor, he shared his strategy of "We will go deeper in the faith. Then, sometime in the fall (of the year), we will focus on evangelism." Sad to say, the evangelistic focus never happened, and the church closed its doors in the next two years. That church believed in the "deeper first" falsehood.

Look at the example of Jesus. His mission included an intentional, continual focus on reaching the unreached from the get-go. He did not operate sequentially by leading with discipleship and then following with evangelism. He did both at the same time. Here's one of Jesus's opening statements to two potential followers: "'Come, follow me,' Jesus said, 'and I will send you out to fish for people'" (Mark 1:17). Jesus included evangelism even before Peter and Andrew signed up. Inviting others into a relationship with Christ is the main thing, not an "also-ran." Sharing your faith remains a primary focus of our lives from the time we experience it.

When I enlisted my youth to help with the Billy Graham Crusade, as I mentioned earlier, one of the sessions included a Q&A time. A participant asked the Billy Graham Evangelistic Association leader why the BGEA did not focus on discipleship. The leader stated, "We have found when you focus on discipleship, you don't do evangelism. But when you focus on evangelism, and people get saved, you learn discipleship to answer the questions new believers have." His insights rang true.

So, what happened to the pastoral candidate mentioned above? The one who espoused "I will lead them to become more like Christ, and then evangelism will happen organically" during his ordination council? He got voted out of his church three years later. There were reasons beyond his misdirected views on evangelism, but the "deeper first" thinking certainly contributed to it. I'm not saying every leader who believes this Ministry Myth will lose their job. Many pastors believe it until they retire. But I am saying this strategy does not work, and Jesus did not subscribe to it. Leaders, don't fall into the trap of thinking people will "organically" share their faith. They need to see you sharing your faith. Plus, they need systems, encouragement, and accountability to do it.

***People need leaders who follow Jesus's strategy.***

## Failed Strategy #3

*We Have to Find the Right Solution.*

"We want to be 100 percent sure this is what God wants us to do," the congregation of thirteen people (average attendance) told me. They asked me to help them figure out how to turn around the decades-old decline of their church. Their attendance peaked at around 150 people about thirty-three years ago. The median age of the current group exceeded sixty years old, the oldest a ninety-year-old church matriarch. Their constitution required nineteen committees (yes, nineteen!). They were obviously in trouble as a congregation. You could see it in the building and hear it in their questions. It's a sad state of affairs to witness a church in decline. Part of the reason for their decline was their belief in the Ministry Myth of the "right solution."

Looking for the "right solution" carries the idea that there is only one right solution. If there is only one right answer, it means all the others are wrong. Even if it were true that there was only one right solution, how in the world would you know it's the right one? The implications don't reveal themselves with any determination until you get a few steps into the decision. So, does the "right solution" mean you won't have to deal with issues? I don't know anything that works like that. What criteria would you use? It's unattainable. If you think there's only one right solution, you stop before you start. You set the bar way too high. In doing so, you absolve yourself of any responsibility to act. If we have to be 100 percent sure of something before we act, we won't ever do it.

Have you ever been 100 percent sure of a decision? I don't think I have. When I look back on even my best decisions, I remember those twinges of doubt and periods of second-guessing that accompanied them. When I moved from a great church in Texas to direct the network of churches, I often woke up at night staring into the dark ceiling. The question that came to mind was, "Am I the dumbest person I ever met for leaving that church and taking over a declining network of churches?" I can tell you when that's your first question, the rest of the internal dialogue does not go in a good direction. Even though I believed God wanted us to move, it was our toughest transition. I wasn't even close to being 100 percent sure that's what we were supposed to do.

What's more, I don't know anyone who was "100 percent sure" of their decision. And, if I am (or could be) 100 percent sure, is that operating according to faith? The great leaders I know don't tell me they are 100 percent sure. They say things like, "I believe God wants us to do this," or "We will try it and trust God to use it." Here's another, "We have prayed, planned, and tried to understand our situation. Now, we will act and trust God." It's the "trust God" part that we miss if we require 100 percent certainty.

*Attempting to find the "right solution" too often results in inactivity and decline.*

Don't fall for this Ministry Myth and miss seeing God do great things through you and your church.

## Failed Strategy #4

*We Don't Use Strategy at Our Church; We Just Follow God.*

In the church where I spent my early years, I heard similar statements: "We don't use strategy at our church; we just follow God." "We just go where the Lord leads; we don't plan." Another leader said, "We don't plan; we just do." One Sunday morning, our pastor even said (from the pulpit, nonetheless), "We don't plan our worship services. But sometimes the music just matches the message as if we had planned it that way." Even as a young adult, I wondered why the pastor didn't plan the service. If it's better when you plan a service to flow well, why not go ahead and plan it?

## Strategy of Avoidance

These statements and their variations may not seem like a strategy. Interestingly enough, this line of thinking forms its own strategy. It's a strategy of avoidance.

The people who say, "We don't plan," in actuality, plan *not* to plan. They set out to not think ahead. Their strategy is to "wing it" when the time comes and see what happens. They strategize not to use strategy.

Unfortunately, many Christian leaders carry this idea. I'm not sure why. They love God and serve Him, but somewhere along the years they adopted this rationale. Some don't like strategy, and others tell me they feel ill-equipped. I've heard people say it's somehow unspiritual. Others may be under the impression that strategy is simply sinful. Many of them lack experience in an effective ministry, so they really aren't sure how to increase their church's impact. Consequently, some seem to operate from the idea that a new initiative needs to be easy or simple. In my work with hundreds of churches, this hesitation to plan or get organized actually prevents what God wants to do.

But you might be wondering, what about the times God miraculously intervenes? For example, what role does strategy play in a large, unforeseen, and unplanned financial donation to the ministry? It's certainly true that something occasionally happens when a church does not plan. Sometimes great things happen when they just show up,

A ministry might receive a windfall donation, or an amazing leader moves into town and joins their church, or the value of their property skyrockets. But these are few and far between. Any one of these things creates less impact when it happens to an organization without a clear strategy.

A few years ago, someone discovered natural gas on several acres of a campground that a Christian ministry owned. The ministry could continue to operate the camp while leasing property to the fracking company. They received a check of almost a million dollars! In addition, they were to receive royalties of thousands of dollars into the future. In talking to one of the key leaders, I asked him if that initial million dollars would help them. He said, "No, not really." He went on to explain what I already knew. Their cash revenue had been decreasing for years, to the point their staffing level was about a fourth of what it was previously. Participation and involvement slid downhill. They did not strategize effectively. In their case, not working a strategy created problems that not even a million dollars could solve.

A soft perusal shows churches that strategize effectively accomplish what God intended. You accomplish more with less effort when you take time on the front end of an endeavor to plan it. Strategize. Figure out the best way to proceed and then go for it. If Jesus, the Son of God, planned, why should we think we should avoid it?

The "We don't use strategy at our church; we just follow God" concept consistently produces lackluster results. Sadly, when churches avoid planning and (predictably) nothing of consequence happens, they falsely conclude, "I guess God didn't want it to happen."

Instead of believing and following Ministry Myths, which regularly fail to meet expectations, let's follow the strategy Jesus used. He did not believe any of these fables. Sadly, many well-intentioned pastors and churches accept these myths as facts. Then, they don't see God do what only God can do. God really does want to work through your church. Pastor, God wants even more for your ministry than you want. The leader who wants to see God move will abandon false thinking and embrace how God works.

How do we know God works strategically? It shows up in the strategy of Jesus, to be sure. But God also shows His organizational strategy, by example, in the way He instructed the church to operate. He set up pastors (local church leaders) to fulfill three sets of expectations. When pastors use all three of these skills, great things happen. These are also the selfsame set of skills every business leader needs. Let's take a look.

*Chapter 5*

# THE THREE SKILLS
# EVERY PASTOR NEEDS

*"The **elders** who are among you I exhort, I who am a fellow **elder** and a
witness of the sufferings of Christ, and also a partaker of the glory that will
be revealed: **Shepherd** the flock of God which is among you, serving as
**overseers**, not by compulsion but willingly, not for dishonest gain but eagerly."*
—1 Peter 5:1–2 (NKJV) (emphasis mine)

The Bible requires three skills to effectively lead a local congregation:
Elder—Shepherd—Overseer. All three are necessary for your church to
do well.

## Elder–Shepherd–Overseer

When I do strategic planning with a church or a company, I request several papers.
Those documents include the job description for the key leader. In a company, it's
typically the CEO. For a church, the key leader is the pastor. The reason to ask
for the pastor's job description is because the church expresses what she wants to
do by the responsibilities given to the key leader. The job description for the main
leader gives a bird's eye view of what that local body of Christ wants to accomplish. It's one way the church expresses her purpose. In a nutshell, the church's

mission (the main part of the purpose) shows what she thinks God wants her to do. As the leader of the organization, the pastor carries the responsibility to fulfill the purpose of the church.

When people ask me what our organization does, I share our mission statement. For the network of churches that I direct, our mission is to "resource, connect, plant, and encourage pastors and churches." It states what the network does and why we exist. But it also says what I am responsible for making sure happens. I don't have to do all the work (and shouldn't), but I am expected to ensure the work of "resource, connect, plant, and encourage pastors and churches" gets done.

Furthermore, each part (resource, connect, plant, and encourage) contains measures. You can see measures. You can count them. It's the yardstick I use to see how well I am performing my job as executive director. As an example, our staff includes a "Pastoral Encourager" to directly fulfill one of our key mandates.

The same is true of a pastor for a church's mission. If your church, as an example, thinks she should "reach people with the gospel, grow them into Christlikeness, and mobilize them to change the world," then that is your job description. If you are the pastor, your job is to make sure your church accomplishes that mission. We know there are tons of things that you do. But in summary, if all those things don't add up to "reach people with the gospel, grow them into Christlikeness, and mobilize them to change the world," you are not fulfilling your responsibility as pastor to your local congregation.

So, how does one go about fulfilling the mission of a church? You fulfill the local church's mission by learning and exercising three skills. The Bible calls them out several times throughout the New Testament. Without these three sets of skills, a pastor will flounder. And, when the pastor struggles, the church struggles. Interestingly, these three sets of skills mirror the skills Jesus used when He started and led the church. Here they are:

1.  Elder
2.  Shepherd (or Pastor)
3.  Overseer (or Bishop)

Some mistakenly say these three words are interchangeable. That is not the case. If they could be substituted for each other, why would the Bible use three different words to describe one office? It doesn't. It wouldn't. The biblical writers use these three words to describe the three functions of the same office. View them not as titles that can be swapped for one another, but instead, see them as three distinct yet overlapping sets of skills you need to lead your church to fulfill her mission. Engage and learn all three to enjoy the ministry and see God work.

## Every Pastor's Three-Part Job Description

*"Qualifications of a pastor: the mind of a scholar,
the heart of a child, and the hide of a rhinoceros."*
—Stuart Briscoe

A friend of mine pastors an ever-growing church, Osborne Baptist Church, in a very unlikely area. It's unlikely because the church has grown in spiritual depth and in the number of people getting saved and attending, while the city itself has stagnated in population. The city of Eden sits in the Piedmont region of North Carolina. Formerly a base for textile mills, the mills (and the last 495 textile jobs) left in 2003, shortly after Pastor Steve Griffith's arrival.

As the church grew, she bought the former headquarters of Fieldcrest, at one time the "largest home textile producer in the world."[11]

In looking at Eden's population over the last three decades, we see the city had 15,238 people in 1990. As of the 2020 census, the town had 15,421,[12] a whopping increase of 183 residents, not much of a bump over a thirty-year period. Conversely, when Pastor Steve arrived at OBC as pastor, the church averaged 128 people weekly. In 2022, post-pandemic, they reach in excess of 1,600 people every week.

Osborne Baptist Church continually increased her impact, attendance, baptisms, and international gospel impact even while the population of her town barely budged. Additionally, not easily seen in the population statistics is the loss of two major employers. Those kinds of losses can devastate a small town whose closest major city sits forty-five minutes away.

In 2021, they sent a couple to plant a church in Los Chiles, Costa Rica, where they had already baptized several new believers through their missions' endeavors.

People's lives literally transform as a result of this church's influence. Marriages get restored. People come out of addiction to live productive, God-honoring lives, and the community receives support. They also partner with mission partners in the United States like Stowe Mission of Central Ohio and a church in Salt Lake City, Utah, in this true multi-generational church.

During the pandemic, they launched a $10 million building project.

How can that happen? Most church leaders know growing churches typically find a home in an area where the population grows. They recognize that people who move to a new area are most likely to connect to a local church. However, Osborne Baptist Church defies conventional wisdom. According to the pastor, they have never had a huge surge in attendance. The increase in ministry happens steadily, adding about a hundred people a year or so by steadily following the strategy Jesus used.

About fifteen years into his pastorate, Pastor Steve's father and mother moved to be closer to him and his family. A Dallas Theological Seminary graduate with a ThM degree, Pastor Dewey (Pastor Steve's father) still does his daily time with the Lord from the Greek New Testament. He watched the incredible growth of OBC for ten years before telling his son, Pastor Steve, "You know, I was always taught if you teach the Bible well, the church will grow. I now see that's not true." Pastor Dewey discovered what he had been taught about leading a church was inaccurate.

The truth is it takes more than biblical preaching to lead a church effectively. If that's all it takes, why aren't all Bible-preaching churches growing? By the way, the Bible teaches that the pastor of a local church needs to do more than preach. At issue is the recognition that the Bible requires three sets of skills for pastors, not one or two.

Here they are:

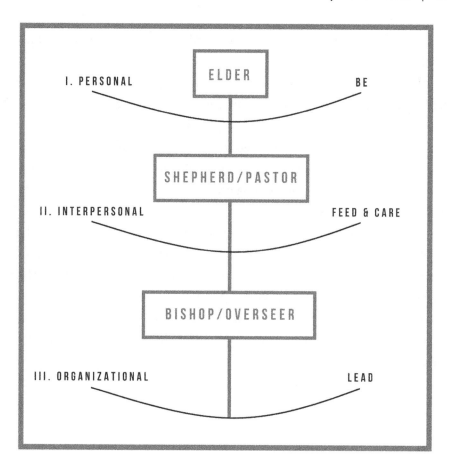

This diagram shows the trine-tiered requirements as the leader of a local congregation. When the Bible uses the word "Elder," it's expecting the leader in a local church to be a person of spiritual and emotional depth. The key issue at the personal level is trustworthiness. A trustworthy pastor possesses integrity, a close walk with Christ, and harbors no known sin. Churches expect pastors to pray, read, and study the Scriptures, pay their bills, and show up to the meetings they schedule.

Secondly, the Bible uses the word "Pastor" or "Shepherd" to show the importance of interpersonal skills. The pastor must love and care for people. The word "shepherd" in its most literal sense means someone who feeds and cares for animals. The shepherd lives with and looks out for livestock. God's Word often describes us this way: "Then we your people, the sheep of your pasture, will praise you forever; from generation to generation, we will proclaim your praise" (Psalm 79:13).

The Bible refers to us as sheep and therefore instructs pastors to care for and feed us. For a pastor, trust stands as the crucial issue. Do your people trust you? Can they relate to you and believe what you say? Trust requires character, but it also requires competence. If my car needs repairs, for example, I may trust you to tell the truth. But if you don't have mechanical skills, I won't let you attempt to fix my vehicle. This caring and feeding necessarily includes preaching ("feeding"), along with pastoral care.

The third skill the Bible requires from the main leader is organizational leadership. The Overseer function is the most often avoided of the lead role (in my experience working with hundreds of churches). As the overseer, the pastor bears responsibility for the enterprise as a whole and the church as an entity. No one else occupies this central place of influence. Surely, other people can help. But if anyone other than the pastor occupies the main Overseer seat, the church will lack the effectiveness she could have.

**Elder + Pastor + Overseer**
**Elder ≠ Pastor ≠ Overseer**

One calling. One job. Three skill sets.

It's one office, the office of the pastor. That one office includes three key functions. These three areas of responsibility describe the three skills all effective leaders must possess. Using these three terms, the Bible shows us the three different levels of effectiveness for the leader who desires to lead well. This means avoiding or denying any one of the three will lessen the impact of the mission Christ entrusted to that local leader. So, biblically, if you are a pastor, fulfilling your role means continually learning to improve as an elder, a pastor, and an overseer. When these three areas improve in sync with the church's purpose, they form a beautifully developing experience of God's grace and love. This symphony of God's love provides a sense of ease and joy in the pastor and an encouraging family for all who participate. It's an incredibly uplifting and fun place to be. It's within the reach of every pastor.

Some churches call the leader "Pastor." Some call the key leader "Elder." Others refer to the leader of the local body of Christ by calling that person "Bishop." Whatever title you use for the main leader/preacher, each church needs all three skills to function well. It's important to note that none of us is naturally gifted in all three areas. I know I'm not. But I do know God can help me learn what I need to know for things to go well. God not only can help you learn, but He wants you to learn *and* develop. He doesn't want you to continue struggling. The God Who called you cares for you. Pastor, the challenges you face today can be overcome. Your church can be a place of healing and grace. This extends not only to the people but also to you.

Furthermore, who you become in the overcoming smooths out your future. Problems become fewer and less intense. More people enjoy serving because they see God at work. Your parishioners smile and are honored to be a part of what only God can do. From my vantage point, there's no better way to live. Once you taste it, you never want to return to the days of frustration.

## Overview of the Three Functions

*"From Miletus he sent to Ephesus and called for the **elders** of the church. And when they had come to him, he said to them: "You know, from the first day that I came to Asia, in what manner I always lived among you […] For I have not shunned to declare to you the whole counsel of God. Therefore, take heed to yourselves and to all the flock, among which the Holy Spirit has made you **overseers**, to **shepherd** the church of God which He purchased with His own blood."*
—Acts 20:17–18, 27–28 (NKJV) (emphasis mine)

**1. Elder.** The word "elder" (*presbuteros* in the Greek New Testament) describes a person who is mature in their faith. It denotes vested authority grounded in the elder's personal adherence to spiritual disciplines. (It does not mean "older" in this instance.) The word "elder" describes the person. An elder knows how to "be" like Christ. This person, as the Bible describes it, retains Christlike character. It's someone who is trustworthy.

The book of Acts identifies elders as leaders. Elders considered matters along with the apostles (Acts 15:6) and led in making decisions with the apostles (Acts 15:22). They are mentioned only secondarily to the apostles in Acts 15:2 and Acts 16:4. Paul also describes elders as church leaders in 1 Timothy 4:14 (CSB): "Don't neglect the gift that is in you; it was given to you through prophecy, with the laying on of hands by the council of elders."

Additionally, the Apostle John calls himself "*The Elder*" in 2 John 1 and 3 John 1. Paul also gave Titus authority to appoint elders in every city (Titus 1:5), as "*I directed you.*" In the local church, those who are sick call for the elders (James 5:14).

So, elders perform a primary role in leading the local church based in no small part on their walk with Christ. As an elder, your primary responsibility is to be formed into the image of Christ, to be like Him. But the Bible does not only want pastors to possess an intimate walk with Christ as elders; it urges us to love those entrusted to our care.

**2. Pastor.** Another word used for the local leadership role in the church is "pastor." The term "pastor" (*poimen* in Greek) means "shepherd." We use the moniker "pastor" so often it's easy to forget it comes to us from a countryside setting. A "pastoral" scene overlooks herds, trees, and greenery away from city life. Likewise, someone who is a pastor connects with, relates to, and lives among the herds. Shepherds must be in contact with the sheep to feed and care for them. In a church, feeding and caring include preaching God's Word and possessing relational warmth, along with interpersonal skills. This means God's shepherd loves, cares for, and relates to God's people, often referred to as sheep. Many use the term "pastor" to describe the leader of the local congregation. Others may use the (entirely legit) title "elder."

Because the local church leader relates to the people, the pastor must possess or acquire interpersonal skills. No matter the pastor's personality, you work with people. No pastor should be a porcupine person, someone "with a few good points but nobody wants to get close to them." One of the most effective pastors I ever met was an introvert. His nature would make you think he would go to his study to be alone right after his sermon. He never did that. That pastor stayed and talked and shared and prayed with people. His personality was introverted, but his calling was pastor. For you, pastor, if you want the church to do well, you must hone and improve your interpersonal skills. You need to be able to provide comfort to people. They should feel relaxed and encouraged around you. One of the notable traits of Jesus was how children loved to be around Him.

Another interpersonal skill required of pastors is the ability to manage conflict. You won't find an effective leader who cannot resolve dissension, large and small. So, the function of shepherd (pastor) goes a level beyond the skills identified with the term "elder." Whereas elder bespeaks the personal spiritual walk of the individual person, the pastor/shepherd title emphasizes the interpersonal connection. You cannot "shepherd" ("pastor") without sheep!

The two roles side-by-side look like this:

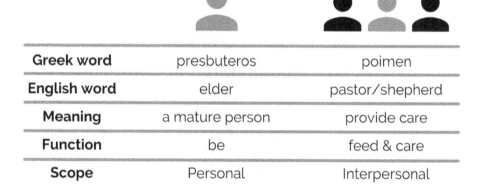

| Greek word | presbuteros | poimen |
|---|---|---|
| English word | elder | pastor/shepherd |
| Meaning | a mature person | provide care |
| Function | be | feed & care |
| Scope | Personal | Interpersonal |

So, the first set of skills belongs to the elder role. A person who is an elder lives a life wholly devoted to Christ. Then, we see pastoral (shepherding) skills in how you relate to other people. But there's a third necessary set of skills a pastor must possess. It's this third set of skills that seems to be lagging in most churches. When I facilitate a strategy of Jesus process with a local church, each key leader takes a "Strategic Leader Assessment." It's a self-evaluation of three areas: elder, pastor, and overseer. So far, every church's weak spot is the skill of overseer, the third of the skills.

**3. Overseer.** From the Greek word *episkopos*, overseer means to "see over." The prefix "epi" means over or above. In the second part of the word *skopos*, you can see telescope, periscope, or microscope. The "scopes" see what cannot be seen with the naked eye. Another English word that means the same as "over" + "seer" is "super + vision." For example, a superscript letter describes a letter or character "above the line." A superscript letter often looks like this number 28 when designating a verse, such as in Acts 20:28: [28]Keep watch over yourselves . . .

"Super" means "above," just as a superscript number is "above the line," while *skopos* means "to see." Periscope, microscope, and telescope all communicate seeing and vision.

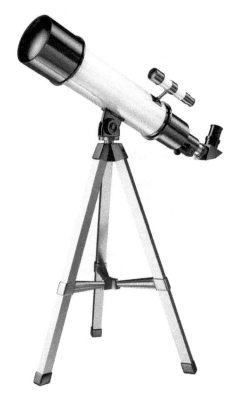

So, an "overseer" is one who "sees over" or "super + "vises" (vision). The pastor holds the responsibility as the main supervisor of the church according to the Bible's usage of the term.

According to the Bible, the lead in the local congregation bears supervisory responsibility, in addition to the personal (elder) and interpersonal (pastor) requirements. Acts 20:28 tells us the Holy Spirit made us "*overseers.*" Paul addresses the book of Philippians to the saints, "including the overseers and deacons." In the clearest and fullest passage about the requirements of the key local leaders, 1 Timothy 3 names the role "overseer" in verses 1 and 2. The word "overseer" or "supervisor" describes the local leader in the following passages:

→ Acts 20:28 (see above).

→ "Paul and Timothy, servants of Christ Jesus, to all the saints in Christ Jesus who are at Philippi, with the overseers and deacons" (Philippians 1:1, ESV).

→ "The saying is trustworthy: If anyone aspires to the office of overseer, he desires a noble task" (1 Timothy 3:1, ESV).

→ "For an overseer, as God's steward, must be above reproach. He must not be arrogant or quick-tempered or a drunkard or violent or greedy for gain" (Titus 1:7, ESV).

→ "Shepherd the flock of God which is among you, serving as overseers, not by compulsion but willingly, not for dishonest gain but eagerly" (1 Peter 5:2, NKJV).

In my limited experience with churches, the overseer function is undervalued at best or ridiculed at worst. People decry "CEO Pastors." Somehow, they believe it is wrong to lead or to give oversight. Yet, biblically, pastors are not only expected but required to perform executive oversight functions. What's more, Jesus certainly did. Later we will see that Jesus clarified the purpose, shared the plan, did the work, formatted the organization (the church), and consistently aligned that group of people to the values He espoused. He admonished Peter. He gave direction to the feeding of the 5,000. He told people what to do. Matthew 14:16 (ESV) gives us but one of the many examples of Jesus directing other people's behavior: "But Jesus said, 'They need not go away; you give them something to eat.'" According to what many churchgoers say, pastors aren't supposed to be giving direction to anybody. That attitude flies in the face of biblical revelation and relegates the church to ineffectiveness.

Additionally, the clearest passage describing the office of the pastor uses the title "overseer." Among the requirements listed for a pastor, 1 Timothy 3 (CSB) includes a management function and a pastor's supervisory expectation.

Let's look at verses 1 through 7.

**Verse 1:** This saying is trustworthy: If anyone aspires to be an overseer, he desires a noble work.

**Verse 2:** An overseer, therefore, must be:

- above reproach
- the husband of one wife
- self-controlled
- sensible
- respectable
- hospitable
- able to teach

**Verse 3:**

- not an excessive drinker
- not a bully but gentle
- not quarrelsome
- not greedy

**Verse 4:** He must manage his own household competently and have his children under control with all dignity.

**Verse 5:** (If anyone does not know how to manage his own household, how will he take care of God's church?)

**Verse 6:** He must not be a new convert, or he might become conceited and incur the same condemnation as the devil.

**Verse 7:** Furthermore, he must have a good reputation among outsiders so that he does not fall into disgrace and the devil's trap.

This grocery list of qualifications for a pastor primarily deals with issues of character, with being "above reproach," "self-controlled," "sensible," and the like indicate the kind of person, or the character qualities, required of a church leader, a pastor. Yet, two items demand "doing." The two areas of doing are "teaching" (verse 2) and "managing" (verses 4 and 5). In my realm, through the years, only teaching was mentioned as something a pastor "does." I heard it again the other day: "The only requirement for a pastor that requires doing is 'able to teach.'" But that's not true. The Bible also requires a management function of a pastor. "He must manage . . ." means the pastor performs an action, a doing. "Manage" is an action word, not a verb of being.

Interestingly enough, each of the "being" requirements only gets a mention, usually just one word, "respectable," "hospitable," etc., which is why I call it a "grocery list." But one of the requirements gets more than a mention. It's the management function. The necessity to manage well occupies two full verses! Verses 4 and 5 tell us a pastor must manage. It also tells us if a pastor cannot manage his own household, he won't be able to take care of the church. From an expository viewpoint, the management function stands alone in the requirements in 1 Timothy 3 as needing two verses to clarify it. Using two verses to describe the management function shows that the Bible gives considerable heft to this foundational skill. Far from just "being," God mandates the pastor to manage and manage effectively.

Good management requires strategy. How do we know it includes strategy? Because of the word "competently." You, as the leader, must not only manage but do so competently (verse 4). God wants us to manage well. The Bible requires you to do a good job of leading. (Management is a function of leadership.) Managing well means you don't just use a program or follow a prescribed process. Managing well means you just don't preach on Sunday morning and hope for the best. Managing strategically means you clearly understand the desired ends, and you can navigate your family or your church to achieve it.

***Biblically, the admonition to manage well is unavoidable.***

So, three functions are required for the leader in a local congregation. These three skills also match the three skills that Jesus used in His strategy. Each of these three functions (elder, pastor, overseer) describes expectations for the leader in the local church. You probably see your own giftedness in one or two. But for the church to be and do all that God desires, all three require high levels of intentionality. The better these three skills, the better the church does. Deny or avoid any one of them to the detriment of what God calls us to do as pastors over a local church or ministers over a particular area within the church or as leaders in business. Embrace all three and you breathe refreshing air to buoy your days and sense God's presence. In reality, for whatever organization or department you lead, working on these three areas will improve your leadership.

From personal experience, when your leadership improves, your life gets better. Even now, I remember the frustration and disappointment of those early days. I'm happy to report that those aggravations are just distant memories. Certainly, I still face challenges from time to time, but nothing like before I changed to become a better elder, shepherd, and overseer. Recently, I texted with a long-time friend. We reminisced about how hard those early days were and contrasted those days with how well things go now, almost effortlessly. The more the ministry expands its depth and impact, the more gratitude I give God for what He is doing. I am so glad I didn't quit when the ministry seemed impossible. Pastor, after over thirty years in ministry, I can tell you what you will experience in the days to come, as you yield and learn more in each of these three areas, is worth it. Hang in there.

| Greek word | presbuteros | poimen | episkopos |
|---|---|---|---|
| English word | elder | pastor/shepherd | bishop/overseer |
| Meaning | a mature person | provide care | supervise, direct |
| Function | be | feed & care | lead |
| Scope | Personal | Interpersonal | Organizational |

# The Pastoral Fallacy

Understanding and fulfilling the threefold responsibility of a pastor answers the question I had in my first church: "I'm preaching and teaching and loving the people and sharing the gospel. So why doesn't my church improve?"

Here's the pastoral fallacy I was taught: "If you walk closely to Christ, believe and teach the Bible, and love your people, God will take care of the church." Notice this fallacy embraces the first two functions of the pastor (elder and shepherd) but totally leaves out the overseer function. A church's ineffectiveness can often be traced to failing to see the church as an organization. I did not know that when I started as a pastor, which led to a lot of heartache.

When a pastor only focuses on developing their own spiritual walk (as an elder) and the relationships with other people (as the pastor/shepherd), they make it well-nigh impossible for the church to get traction. For the church to be effective, a pastor must lead the church as a whole and not just a bucket of parts.

Sometimes the pastor thinks it is unspiritual to oversee the church. Very often, the people in the church believe the pastor should only do "churchy" things like marry, bury, and be a missionary. They too often rail against the pastor setting a direction, establishing a plan for which they are accountable, or removing a volunteer who isn't getting the job done. Church members rarely connect the dots between leading the church as a whole and the church becoming more effective.

You'll hear the Pastoral Fallacy in statements like:

"If God wants it to grow, it will grow."

"We just do our part and leave the rest up to God."

"We need to gain a consensus before we move forward."

"Our church focuses on unity."

"We don't follow preachers; we just follow the Lord."

To see what this looks like, refer to the diagram on the next page.

These sayings may sound spiritual to some people. I'm not sure why. The Bible does not support these proclamations. But the Pastoral Fallacy not only shows up in what people say, but it's also evident in how a church does the work of a church. Here are some possible indicators your church is not functioning as a whole.

## Possible Indicators of the Presence of the Pastoral Fallacy

→ It takes two steps to get something done, which could be done in one step. But "so everyone knows what's going on," or "to include everyone,"

# PASTORAL FALLACY

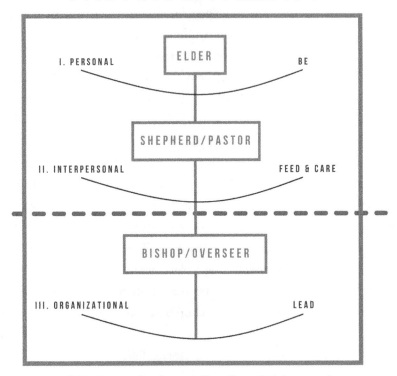

I. PERSONAL     ELDER     BE

SHEPHERD/PASTOR

II. INTERPERSONAL     FEED & CARE

BISHOP/OVERSEER

III. ORGANIZATIONAL     LEAD

"If I do well above the line (elder and pastor), God will take care of the church (overseer) below the line."

or "to go through the necessary groups/boards/committees," you take two (or more) steps.

➤ Committees meet regularly. This author defines a committee as "a group of people deciding what somebody else should or could be doing." If committees meet regularly, the people think they do ministry because they sit on a committee. Committees necessarily mean it will take longer to do anything because after the committee decides, the verdict needs to be communicated to the people doing the ministry. Then the person doing the ministry must navigate the decision among their area of ministry, for good or for ill. A good overseer realizes God is not honored because you unnecessarily take up people's time to get things done.

→ Congregational votes are expected (or required) on things like the times of your services, electing people to teach/lead a small group, maintenance/repair issues, and small purchases.

→ Your church talks a lot about the pastor being a "shepherd" but refuses to acknowledge them as a leader.

→ Your church cares more about the process of reaching a decision than they care about the effectiveness of the decision.

→ Your church's leaders (the ones doing the ministry) do not meet or meet less than once a month to plan. You can certainly meet without leading. But it is impossible to lead without meeting. When do you lead? It happens when you are with the leaders in a room, determining the ministries' overall direction and next steps. When a church's leaders do not regularly connect on mission and direction, the church flounders.

Your church can avoid the negative results (waning participation, time spent in meetings, lack of effectiveness) of the Pastoral Fallacy by following the strategy of Jesus. Jesus used an organizational strategy to lead the church as a whole organization. But Jesus began with a personal strategy.

*Chapter 6*

# JESUS'S PERSONAL STRATEGY
# –LUKE 2:52

*"Jesus grew in wisdom and in stature and in favor with God and all the people."*
—Luke 2:52 (NLT)

our personal habits, attitudes, and beliefs show up and get bigger in the organization you lead. This includes a pastor and a church.

## Purpose and Personal Direction

*"The Son of Man came to seek and to save the lost."*
—Luke 19:10

Jesus's leadership strategy began with His personal strategy, the first sphere. His personal strategy begins with His personal purpose. That's why "Personal Purpose" sits at the very center (in the middle circle) of the strategy of Jesus. His purpose (and yours) gives direction to every other area of your life, including the church (or organization) you work for or lead. The word the Bible uses most prominently for purpose (*prothesis*) means 1. the setting forth of a thing, placing of it in view and 2. a purpose.[13] Prothesis is used in Romans 8:28, "And we know that in all things God works for the good of those who love Him, who have been called according to His purpose."

The same word is used to describe bread put aside for a particular reason, consecrated, in Matthew 12:4: "He entered the house of God, and he and his companions ate the consecrated bread—which was not lawful for them to do, but only for the priests." In the English Standard Version, it's called the "bread of the Presence." God sets you apart, and His Presence accompanies you, evidenced by your unique, one-of-a-kind purpose.

But your purpose only guides you if you know what it is and if you make decisions based on it. In Jesus's case, God clarified His purpose before He was born. In Matthew 1:21 (ESV), an angel of the Lord appeared to Joseph and told him the purpose of Christ's birth: "She will bear a son, and you shall call his name Jesus, for he will save his people from their sins." That is why Jesus came. Just like Jesus, your personal purpose occupies the central place to tutor you to live a life well-lived. It's the centerpiece around which everything else flows. Here's how the personal strategy of Jesus looks:

## JESUS'S PERSONAL STRATEGY

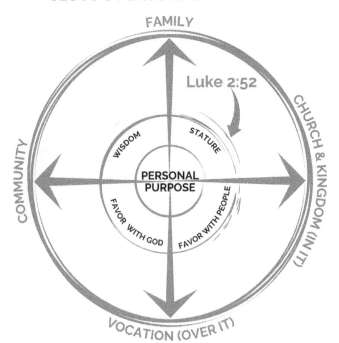

Multiple times in the Old Testament and the New, God made sure we knew why He sent His son, what He came to earth to do. From the first book of the Bible, we find the first indication of Jesus's purpose. Known as the protevange-lium, or "first gospel" (*prota* [first] + *euangelion* [gospel]), Genesis 3:15 (ESV) states: "I will put enmity between you and the woman, and between your off-spring and her offspring; he shall bruise your head, and you shall bruise his heel." It's the first indication that Jesus will come to defeat the devil with His sinless life, substitutionary death, and resurrection from the dead.

Then the New Testament also shows Jesus knew why He was here. He shared it. A lot. He communicated His personal purpose with others in "conversations." By my count, Jesus participated in 358 conversations[14] in the gospels. Sometimes a conversation was just a sentence or so ("But Jesus answered him, 'Let it be so now, for thus it is fitting for us to fulfill all righteousness'" (Matthew 3:15, ESV, with John the Baptist). Other times, He conversed for entire chapters (Matthew 5–7, the Sermon on the Mount). In these numerous conversations, Jesus told other people why He was here and what He was to do. In the gospel of Matthew, 44 per-cent of His conversations included a statement about why He was here. In the gos-pels as a whole, 36 percent of Jesus's conversations included His personal purpose.

Sometimes, Jesus Himself said why He was here. Mark 1:38 (ESV) says, "And he said to them, 'Let us go on to the next towns, that I may preach there also, for that is why I came out.'" At other times, someone else named it and Jesus accepted their attribution. For example, in Matthew 8:29, two demon-possessed men cried, "What do you want with us, Son of God?" In that instance, like many others, Jesus did not correct the assertion that He was the Son of God. Although more passive than Jesus stating it directly, it still shows the clarity Jesus possessed about why He came.

## Why Talk About Our Purpose?

So, here's the question for us. Why did Jesus share His raison d'être so often? What motivated Him to talk about His personal purpose in over a third of the recorded conversations He had with people in the Gospels? Surely, He wanted other people to know. Yet some of these people were in several conversations. I believe He told His purpose not only so other people would know but so that

He would keep clear on it Himself. When you look at all Jesus faced and how many people pulled at Him for healing, to argue, to cast out demons, and to help people, it would be way too easy to get lost along the way.

A second reason I believe Jesus shared His purpose so often was to cue us. Not only does Jesus know His reason for being, but we as His followers should also know ours. Since Jesus knew His purpose and talked about it regularly, so should I. As His personal purpose gave Him direction, my purpose grants me a pathway every day. My mission is to "develop leaders to achieve kingdom results personally and in the organizations they lead." It guides my annual goals, oversees my quarterly check-ins, gives direction to my daily planning, and also informs how I react in the moment. As a follower of Christ, my purpose reflects Jesus's purpose, but the two are not identical.

## We Each Have a Unique Purpose

To take it a step further, we all don't have the same purpose. When the subject of "what's your purpose" arises, many pastors respond, "My purpose is to glorify God and enjoy Him forever." Or sometimes people say, "Glorify God." As believers, we certainly should glorify God, but "glorify God" isn't our purpose. It's the answer to the question, "What is the chief end of man?"

The first question in the Westminster Shorter Catechism is not asking about your purpose. It asks, "What does it all add up to?" In other words, when you discover and live your purpose, it aggregates to glorifying God. Whereas the "chief end" summarizes your life, your purpose (should) defines your life. Your purpose individually fits you. No two purposes are identical. You can glorify God as a mechanic or a pastor, homemaker, or executive director. Since that's true, what is the path for you to glorify God? What's your individual purpose that factors into the larger whole?

## Eli and Nacho Libre

> *"I am the gatekeeper of my own destiny,*
> *and I will have my glory day in the hot sun."*
> —Nacho Libre

My grandson Eli faces continuous challenges because of SMA2. Spinal Muscular Atrophy Type-2 occurs because a weird gene does not make enough of a protein needed for the motor neurons to work normally. The motor neurons break down and can't send signals to the muscles. So his brain works well (he's very intelligent and kind of ornery) and his muscles *could* work. But because the motor neuron linkage is broken, every muscle in his body lacks strength. Fortunately, due to medications, he can move his hands enough to operate his "engine" (electric wheelchair) and lift his head if it doesn't fall too far forward. But he could not even manage those functions until recently.

Before these recently discovered meds, Eli landed in the ICU at the local children's hospital when he was three years old. His condition required a ventilator for eight days. Heartrending. After clearing my calendar with the church where I was scheduled to do leadership development, my family and I maintained a vigil throughout the horrible, terrifying limbo, not knowing if he would make it or not. It wrecked me.

When Eli finally got out of the hospital, he did not want to eat. Any kind of food up to this point in his little life usually choked him because his internal musculature lacked the strength necessary to direct the food where it needed to go. He was already emaciated, but the hospital stay further lowered his weight.

So, what do you do to get him to eat?

You show him and his brother Luke the movie *Nacho Libre*.

That's what I did, anyway.

In the movie, the actor Jack Black plays the part of a monk/cook named Ignacio at a Mexican monastery. Later in the movie, Ignacio moonlights as a luchador (Mexican professional wrestler) to earn money to feed the orphans. Since he knew the monastery viewed wrestling as a "sin of vanity," Ignacio fought with the stage name "Nacho" to hide his identity, which forms the title of the movie.

Early on, Ignacio ("Nacho") stays frustrated at the lack of money for food for the orphans the monastery cares for. For example, to get the chips he serves at lunch every day, Ignacio traveled to town on a bicycle each night and gathered the leftovers in the alley behind one of the town's eateries. One night, as he was collecting the chips for the next day's midday meal, Ignacio got jumped by a kid who stole the chips.

Then, lunch the next day finds "Nacho" ladling gruel into the bowls of each of his fellow monks. He's slinging the slop while they stare with defeated disbelief. Probably the oldest monk in the place then raises his hands and says, "Silence, brothers! This is the worst lunch I ever had."

Another brother monk laments: "Where are the spices?" "Where are the cheeps (chips)?"

Nacho replied, "Somebody stole the cheeps."

The brother comes back, "Did you not tell him these are the Lord's cheeps?"

I used that scene to show a bag of Nacho Cheese Doritos to my grandson Eli. "Hey, Eli! These are Nacho Cheese Doritos. In this bag are the Lord's cheeps. Do you want some?"

He said yes! And he ATE them!

Eli still eats those chips. And we still call them "the Lord's cheeps" at our house.

In the movie, before the lunch scene, ole Nacho shares a version of his own personal purpose: "I am the gatekeeper of my own destiny, and I will have my glory day in the hot sun." Nacho fulfilled his personal purpose by serving the orphans and becoming a luchador to help. Interestingly, the *Nacho Libre* movie is loosely based on the story of Fray Tormenta ("Friar Storm," a.k.a. Rev. Sergio Gutiérrez Benítez), a real-life Mexican Catholic priest who had a twenty-three-year career as a masked luchador and competed in order to support the orphanage he directed.[15]

Whatever we can say about Nacho, he possessed a clear, compelling personal purpose: "Feed orphans and raise money as a luchador to do it." Then he did it. As it is for Nacho, so it is for you, my friend.

Get clear on why you are on the planet. Then fulfill it. And that's how to experience a life well-lived. Jesus started His strategy by knowing why He was here. Likewise, the strategy of Jesus in your life begins with your personal life purpose.

What about you?

Why are you here?

What motivates you each morning and drives your decisions each day?

Nacho knew and lived His purpose. But Jesus did, too. Jesus possessed a clear personal purpose before He was born physically.

You also have a purpose on this planet, by the way. And, you can know what it is.

# How to Find Your Personal Purpose

*"The two most important days in a person's life are*
*the day they were born and the day they find out why."*
—Mark Twain

God is working in your life right now! He has been working since you were born and even before you were born. Josh Shortridge is a young man who has worked with me for the last nine years at our inner-city ministry. Josh's birth mom wanted his first and middle names to be "Jesse James." As you may know, Jesse James was the name of a notorious outlaw. Jesse James and his gang of thugs robbed banks, stagecoaches, and trains in the mid-1800s. They were also accused of committing atrocities against people, engaging in a life of crime, and recruiting other people into various gangs over the years. Not a bright outlook, especially since James was dead by the age of thirty-four.

But the young man who works with me was not named Jesse James. Right after he was born, his grandfather, who was neither a follower of Jesus nor a student of the Bible, insisted his name be "Joshua Michael." The name "Joshua" comes from the Hebrew and is the equivalent of the New Testament name "Jesus." Furthermore, "Michael" is the name of the only archangel mentioned in the Bible (Revelation 12:7). Because of his background, this young man faced numerous uphill battles in his younger years. But Joshua Michael came to be a trusted, respected leader in the nonprofit sector, reaching many for the cause of Christ. God worked in Joshua's life even before he was old enough to realize it. The same is true for all of us.

God wants us to know our purpose. In the Bible, the Apostle Paul prayed it for the church at Colossae: "And so, from the day we heard, we have not ceased to pray for you, asking that you may be filled with the knowledge of his will in all spiritual wisdom and understanding" (Colossians 1:9, ESV). Jeremiah, the biblical prophet, also knew this: "For I know the plans I have for you, declares the Lord, plans for welfare and not for evil, to give you a future and a hope" (Jeremiah 29:11, ESV).

Furthermore, the Apostle Paul said God designed a plan for him from the time he took his first breath: "But when God, who set me apart from my mother's womb and called me by his grace, was pleased to reveal his Son in me so that I might preach him among the Gentiles" (Galatians 1:15–16).

God also wants you to know. Many factors influence your life. Put together, five key areas form your personal purpose, your reason for being on the planet:

1. **Your History:** What has God done in your life until now?
2. **Mission:** What does God want from you?
3. **Your Passion:** What do you like doing? Do you work better with people? Things? Ideas? God planted that passion in you because He wants it to be expressed through you.
4. **Your Inclination:** What are your skills, abilities, strengths, and spiritual gifts?
5. **Your Contribution:** What does the world need? People may already see a need for what you have to give. Or it may be that the world does not yet see what you will create that people will need. Nobody thought they needed a mobile phone because they had never seen one. Yours may be the next unrealized need in the world.

Here are three methods you can use to unearth your reason for being:

**Method #1:** Write everything you want to do, all you want to be, and everything you want to have in the next ten years. I heard this idea at a Zig Ziglar conference in Houston. Get a legal pad and just write until you cannot think of any other things you want to do, be, and have. Then leave it alone for twenty-four hours or so. Go back and write more. Write until there's no more to write. After you have everything down, group the items into no more than five groups. Name each group. Then combine the five headings into a sentence of around thirteen words about where you are headed.

**Method #2:** Use a Perspective Exercise (accessed free at LeaderIncrease.com). Then aggregate your insights into the single sentence mentioned in Method #1. You choose the answers to the Perspective Exercise because it's a direct expression of the history, mission, passion, inclination, and contribution God planted and nourishes in your heart.

**Method #3:** Enlist the help of someone with expertise in helping leaders take the next step in their personal and professional development, often called an executive coach or a life coach.

Finding your purpose does not have to be a lifelong odyssey of wondering why you're here. You can know. The sooner you know, the clearer life will be.

---

Life by itself does not give clarity.
It's the clarity that gives you life.

---

## Get Clear on Your Purpose, Then Develop Four Areas

*"It's never too late to be who you might have been."*
—George Eliot

Using Jesus's strategy begins with clarifying your personal purpose. Then you must increase in four key areas, the way Jesus did. The New Living Translation says it like this: "Jesus grew in wisdom and in stature and in favor with God and all the people" (Luke 2:52).

Jesus focused on four areas of development.

1. Wisdom (mentally)
2. Stature (physically)
3. Favor with God (spiritually)
4. Favor with people (socially/emotionally)

Out of all Jesus could have done, He chose only these four. His example should be my example. The divine Son of God, originator of the largest organization on the planet today, used this personal tetrad as a framework for personal development, resulting in massive kingdom advancement. No better rubric exists for you to use. The personal strategy of Jesus should be yours and mine.

Each of these elements—wisdom (mental development), stature (physical improvement), favor with God (spiritual depth), and favor with people (emotional/social health)—represents a necessary aspect of your personal growth and leadership.

The Yale professor Henry Burt Wright, in his 1909 work *The Will of God and a Man's Lifework*, called it "The Fourfold Touchstone of Jesus and the Apostles." He says the greatest commandment lines up exactly with Jesus's personal strategy.

"The most important one," answered Jesus, "is this: 'Hear, O Israel: The Lord our God, the Lord is one. Love the Lord your God with all your heart and with all your soul and with all your mind and with all your strength.' The second is this: 'Love your neighbor as yourself.' There is no commandment greater than these" (Mark 12:29–31).

To Wright:

→ All your heart = socially
→ All your soul = spiritually
→ All your mind = mentally
→ All your strength = physically

Comparing Jesus's strategy with the greatest commandment shows us that the personal strategy of Jesus is not just an example. It's a command.

Let's review how each one contributes to our effectiveness in the following four chapters.

# Chapter 7

# WISDOM—MENTAL DEVELOPMENT

*"Search for wisdom as you would search for silver or hidden treasure."*
—Proverbs 2:4 (CEV)

## Middle School Moxie

The principal of a middle school could not get the girls to stop kissing the mirror in the school bathroom. The greasy lip prints created a lot of unnecessary work for the school's janitor. The principal heard about it way too often. To address the problem, she called the girls into the bathroom along with the janitor who had to do the cleaning. She explained how difficult it was to get lipstick off the mirror. Then she asked the janitor to show what he had to do to clean the mirror. The janitor then dipped his brush into the toilet to wet it. Then he wiped the mirror clean. The girls never kissed the mirror again.

As these girls learned, an increase in information and wisdom led to a change in choices and behavior. How many leaders are kissing the mirror because they don't have the necessary information and wisdom?

***Every leadership position requires wisdom.***

Wisdom operates in the margins of life. You tap wisdom when the first answer looks fuzzy. Wisdom, pictured as a woman in the biblical book of Proverbs, doesn't crave attention or center stage. Rarely is she jarring, except to those who recognize depth. Flashy and splashy are not two words that describe her. Wisdom fits the space between what is known and unknown.

There are things in life that are certain and things in life that are new, if only to me. Wisdom is in the middle. She resides in the "in-between" places, between God's known revealed truth and the wonderment of a unique or particular situation, never encountered in this context with your hard-wiring and this specific group of people. Each new setting is different from any other on earth. Although many similarities to past experiences may exist, it has never been you, never been this exact situation, and it has never been now. Enter wisdom.

Wisdom lists first in Jesus's list of pursuits: "And Jesus increased in wisdom and stature" (Luke 2:52, NKJV). As you acquire wisdom, she guides, instructs, upholds, and supports all the other areas of life personally (physical, favor with God, and favor with people) and organizationally (purpose, plan, work, format, and improvement). Rooted in the fear of the Lord (Proverbs 9:10), wisdom requires a surrender, an acquiescence to what is. Wise people do not violate foundational principles; they adjust their thinking to embrace and apply them, usually in new ways for a given situation.

Acquiring wisdom is a lifelong pursuit. We can get it from others, from the Lord, and even figure it out for ourselves. Wisdom existed before the world began (Proverbs 8:22). As a matter of note, God used wisdom to create the world. Since God used wisdom to make the world, it makes sense that the wiser we become, the more we understand the world: how people, processes, and organizations function. The better you understand wisdom, the greater your comprehension of the Creator and the things He created as well as how they operate in relationship to each other.

## How Do We Know If a Decision Is Wise?

Twice, the book of Proverbs shows us a wisdom trifecta, a threefold test to help us arrive at a wise decision.

*"To receive the instruction of wisdom, justice, judgment, and equity."*
—Proverbs 1:3 (NKJV)

*"Then you will understand righteousness and justice,*
*Equity and every good path."*
—Proverbs 2:9 (NKJV)

A biblical commentator explains it like this:

*"So, the disciple of Proverbs will acquire discipline that will produce*
*a prudent life, and that prudent life will be demonstrated by*
*'doing what is right and just and fair.'"*
—Tremper Longman III, Proverbs—*The Expositor's Bible Commentary*

Wisdom views the world through God's lens. It's seeing the way God sees. Making wise decisions encompasses (as much of) the totality of a situation, applies biblical principles, and then makes a move. Although difficult to categorize, here are three helpful questions to make wise decisions:

## Is the Decision:

1. Right?
2. Proper and fitting (just)?
3. Fair?

### 1. Is It Right?

"Right" means "conformity to a standard, as in Deuteronomy 25:15, where weights and measures were required to be right. The religious use of the term signifies what is right according to the standard of God's law."[16]

We describe the Bible as the "Canon" of Scripture. This "canon" comes from the Hebrew word *qaneh*, which means a "reed" or "measuring rod." The referenced reed served as a measure, much like we use a ruler today. Can you imagine trying to build a house where no two measuring tapes had precisely the same length for inches or feet?

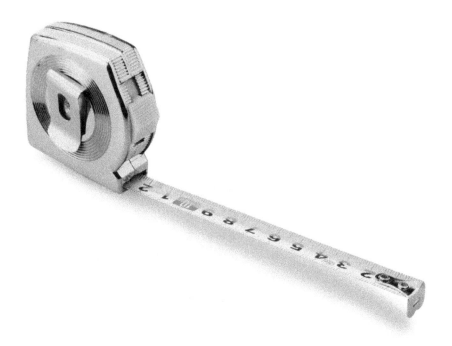

When the house is first being built, the framing carpenter will leave an opening for the window based on his measuring tape. But if the installer used a different measure than the framer, none of the windows would fit! You cannot build a house unless all the builders use the same standard. No wise builder would use two sets of measures. Likewise, no wise believer uses two sets of measurements. We use the measure of God's Word to determine what is "right." A decision, to be wise, requires truth.

This "rightness" forms the overlay for any wise decisions. Some decisions are clearly moral in nature. A wrong moral decision commits sin, and it's inherently unethical and wrong. Lying and stealing are two examples of actions that are not right. Both are immoral according to God's law (Exodus 20:15–16). So a decision that includes lying or stealing cannot be wise.

When there is a choice between right and wrong, the wise person chooses the right.

But not all decisions are moral decisions. How much should I tip the pizza delivery guy? What passage of Scripture should I preach this week? What should I wear to the wedding? What kind of car should I buy? Should I plant a garden this year? What should I do about the person who is fomenting dissension in the church?

For these kinds of decisions, and there are many of them, wisdom needs an additional perspective. This can come from a second question:

## 2. Is It Fitting or Proper?

Proverbs tells us a wise decision is not only right but "just." "Just" connotes that which is fitting or proper. "(Using) Proverbs will develop a life that has a sense of propriety in making decisions."[17]

Finding the fitting answer can be more difficult than finding what is right. Right and wrong tend to be more clear-cut than what decision best "fits." Furthermore, what fits in one situation won't fit best in another. To make matters more complicated, we bring our own sense of decorum to decisions. Past experiences, personality type, culture, and emotional conditioning all affect how we view what is happening.

Understanding that our perceptions affect us, a wise person considers her filters. But she also seeks to understand the preconditioned outlooks of the other people involved. Your wisdom must include metacognition, which is how you think about thinking. Growing wiser means not only looking outside; it includes an analysis of your internal predispositions.

For example, a young man just met his biological father at age eighteen. He spent a weekend with him for the first time. That experience and the accompanying emotions consumed him. Questions about himself and his past, along with what this meant for the days to come, rattled his world. As this almost grown guy relayed the interaction, he commented, "He (his biological father) has sixty-three felony convictions, but he is a nice guy." That's what he said: sixty-three felony convictions! Any one of those qualifiers (sixty-three or felony) or the subject (convictions) would be bad. But this guy just discovered his father, whom he did not know previously, had all three. Yet, even with this knowledge, he described the father as a "nice guy."

Just like that young man, all of us "see through a glass, darkly" (1 Corinthians 13:12, KJV). When you identify and recognize your filters and how those filters affect you, your wisdom increases. Deny them, and your wisdom decreases. Wise people recognize their filters and the effect those filters have on decision-making. Then they choose a fitting decision.

So, if a decision isn't morally wrong and is fitting, it should be wise, right? Not yet. Even when what we are doing is not morally wrong and is fitting or proper, there's a third question to apply to help our decisions to be wise.

"And the wise heart will know the proper time and procedure" (Ecclesiastes 8:5).

### 3. Is It Fair?

Fair ("equity") can describe that which is pleasing (Judges 14:3, "right" [NIV] or "pleases" [NKJV]). Wise decisions please those involved, as far as it is possible. God acts like this. "He rules the world in righteousness and judges the peoples with equity" (Psalm 9:8).

Another translation says it like this: "And He will judge the world in righteousness; He will execute judgment for the peoples fairly" (Psalm 9:8, NASB).

When a decision pleases others, wisdom not only arrives at a good destination, but it makes the trip as enjoyable as possible. Galatians 6:1 (NASB) bears this out when you confront a brother or sister caught in any wrongdoing. When you see someone close to you doing wrong, you "restore such a person in a spirit of gentleness" (Galatians 6:1, NASB). Hard situations do not justify hard handling. The opposite is true if you are wise.

Is it Right? Is it Fitting? Now, make it Fair. Two factors increase the likelihood of a fair decision. Both are possible, even though they are sometimes difficult to find. Those two defining characteristics of fairness are: Does the decision please, and does the decision ease?

## A Closer Look at the Two Defining Characteristics of Fairness

### 1. Does it Please?

A wise decision arrives at an outcome that pleases those involved. This does not mean everybody will like it. But it does mean wise decisions produce wise endings. When a wise person sees a decision coming, she will let it percolate longer to make it as pleasing as possible, given the variables at play. Chasing "pleasing" becomes more important with more difficult and painful situations.

The New Living Translation from 1996 says it like this: "The wise person makes learning a joy" (Proverbs 15:2, NLT).

And the New American Standard Bible says, "The tongue of the wise makes knowledge pleasant" (Proverbs 15:2, NASB).

Here's a question to make your decisions wiser: How can I make this hard decision without being hard toward those living with it?

***A wise choice has the ring of truth.***

When a decision is fair (pleasing, as used here), most people will say, "That makes sense." They mean that considering the variables at work, the solution creates a positive endorsement among the majority of people involved. When this happens, people not only accept the decision, they get behind it. It's a principle I share when working with Pastor Search Teams. When a church's pastor goes to another church or retires, churches often assemble Pastor Search Teams. These teams are tasked with finding the next senior pastor. There's a lot to the process. But one thing I urge them to consider is the idea of making a choice that is pleasing. "You don't want to recommend someone as the next senior pastor who is acceptable. You want to find a candidate everyone (unanimously) on the Pastor Search Team is excited about presenting. It's a tall order, for sure. But I believe it's the path of wisdom."

## 2. Does it Ease?

So, to be fair, the decision must be pleasing. But a wise, fair decision must also ease the pain, even in (and especially in) difficult circumstances. "Does the decision ease?" comes from an entirely different viewpoint than "the truth hurts" crowd.

You recognize them. "Well, the truth hurts, so . . ." is how the discussion starts. Then people get hurt. They probably told the truth, but they certainly were not wise. This group does not give a second thought to hurting people. Somehow, since they are "right," they think it's okay to offend people. They carry a false belief that just because something is "right," it does not need to be "fitting" or "fair." By the way, do you know how to know when someone is about to offend you? They open with, "I don't mean to offend you, but . . ." When somebody says, "I don't mean to offend you, but . . ." they might as well just say, "I'm going to offend you." Because they will. This approach lacks wisdom. I don't know where the "they did wrong, so it's okay to blast them" mentality comes from. I only know it does not come from the Bible.

If you go into a conversation thinking, "the truth hurts," then you pretty much guarantee you will hurt other people. But if, on the other hand, you determine you will create a pleasing experience, no matter how painful it may be, you take one step closer to being wise. Painful issues are painful enough without adding to the pain.

So, how can you take the sting out?

One way to reduce the pain is to love the other person, no matter what they did to hurt you or others. Isn't that what Jesus teaches when He says, "But to you who are willing to listen, I say, love your enemies! Do good to those who hate you. Bless those who curse you. Pray for those who hurt you" (Luke 6:27–28, NLT). Elsewhere, Jesus says, "Love your enemies and pray for those who persecute you, so that you may be sons of your Father who is in heaven" (Matthew 5:44–45, ESV). When a hard decision comes from somebody who loves you, suddenly the decision does not feel quite so hard. Wise people recognize that they do not have to be hard, even when the decision is.

## Still Not Sure If What You Are Thinking Is Wise?

Making decisions as a leader carries an enormous amount of complexity. But it's those moments where leadership earns her stripes. The more wisdom you bring to problems, the more credibility people grant you. Bring a great result now and you increase your leadership momentum to face the next one. Fumble the ball here and the next problem becomes more difficult to solve.

Here's a biblical checklist. I use it when I'm contemplating how best to handle a problem. Is the decision I am about to make "wisdom from above"? If so, is what I'm thinking:

➙ first pure
➙ then peaceable
➙ gentle
➙ willing to yield
➙ full of mercy
➙ full of good fruits

→ without partiality

→ without hypocrisy (James 3:17, NKJV)?

Jesus increased in wisdom. Among the four things Jesus pursued, wisdom comes first. The stronger your wisdom, the better every other part of your life, personally and organizationally, will be.

> *"Wisdom is the principal thing; Therefore, get wisdom."*
> —Proverbs 4:7 (NKJV)

# Seven Proven Ways to Increase Wisdom

Wisdom makes us more effective leaders. We overcome challenges better, accomplish more, and with it enjoy enhanced relationships. Without wisdom, we make bad decisions that cost us stress, time, money, relationships, and wasted opportunities. I continually strive to increase it in my life.

Here are seven ways I acquire more wisdom. I believe they can help you:

## 1. Ask God for it.

God hears this prayer from me more than any other. I rely on James 1:5, "If any of you lacks wisdom, you should ask God, who gives generously to all without finding fault, and it will be given to you." For years now, I say something like: "Dear Lord, if there's one thing I know, it's that I lack wisdom. Please give it to me. Please GRANT it to me. I not only want it, I NEED IT to do what I believe you want me to do."

That's it. I ask. God tells us if we don't have it, just ask for it. You can ask right now.

## 2. Adjust the way you come out and go in.

> *"Now give me wisdom and knowledge, that I may go out and come in*
> *before this people; for who can judge this great people of Yours?"*
> —2 Chronicles 1:10 (NKJV)

When you change the way you enter a room, you change the room. And the room change then should change how you engage, thus creating wisdom. Try it. Walk into a room slowly, shoulders slumped, avoid eye contact, and focus on finding a seat. Then notice how the people in the room respond.

Next, enter room #2 with head held high. Smile, make eye contact, and greet every person in the room with a handshake and a "Hey!" Then make mental notes of what just happened. Room #1 feels like a different world from Room #2 because you adjusted the way you went in. Solomon's prayer included this very awareness because wisdom recognizes (and adjusts) that your coming and going affects the room itself.

## 3. Formally gather others' input.

*"A wise person will hear and increase in learning*
*and a person of understanding will acquire wise counsel."*
—Proverbs 1:5 (NASB)

This means I initiate asking others for wisdom. I don't expect others to invite me to learn. Regularly, I find people who know more than I do about a given subject. Once I discover them, I invite them to breakfast or lunch and ask them questions about that particular subject. With pen in hand, I take notes on their answers. I did this yesterday with Rick Alvis, CEO of Wheeler Mission, in Indianapolis. He leads an incredible ministry to that large city's homeless population. Wheeler Mission went from one location when he started to ten locations now. During his tenure, the mission's income increased twenty-one-fold. They use over 30,000 volunteers. Mind-blowing. I soaked in everything he said, as did the two people I brought with me. We debriefed on the two-and-a-half-hour trip back. My head still swirls, connecting what he said with what I am doing and what I could be doing. This happened because I asked him. I'm wiser for it.

## 4. Ratchet up your discretion by three levels.

How in the world can I increase my discretion by three levels? I increase my wisdom by changing my perspective. "Does not wisdom cry out, and understanding lift up her voice? She takes her stand on the top of the high hill, beside the way, where the paths meet. She cries out by the gates, at the entry of the city, at the entrance of the doors" (Proverbs 8:1–3, NKJV).

Notice the Bible pictures wisdom as a woman, never as a man. Wisdom gets on the top of the heights to acquire a different position physically. She knows a higher position grants an improved perspective. My coach, Terry Walling, says, "The difference between leaders and followers is perspective. The difference between good leaders and great leaders is a better perspective." Wisdom agrees. She looks *at* the path, not *from* the path.

You ratchet up your discretion by three levels when you elevate your perspective. Sometimes called "balcony thinking," wisdom leaves the jostling from the ballroom floor. She ascends the stairs and peers from the balcony at that same scene. A bird's-eye view sees connections and patterns you cannot know from eye-level looking. Wisdom takes three steps up; knowing better perspective brings better solutions.

Or here's another question that helps me get three levels higher: I ask myself, "What would a great leader do in this situation?" Not, "What would I do?" But what would a world-class leader do? Pick a world-class leader of your choice. Then do what that leader would do. This simple question increased my wisdom in dealing with a seemingly impossible situation. It can help you, too.

## 5. Reckon the proper place of pain.

The biblical book of James pictures pain as a mathematical equation. "Count it all joy, my brothers, when you meet trials of various kinds, for you know that the testing of your faith produces steadfastness. And let steadfastness have its full effect, that you may be perfect and complete, lacking in nothing. If any of you lacks wisdom . . ." (James 1:2–5, ESV).

Accounting uses the term "Count it" in verse two. It's a straightforward calculation, and the sum of the equation is "joy." Just as $1 + 1 = 2$, pain equals joy, or at least it does for someone who is wise. Sounds crazy, I know. But that's how wisdom works.

See the passage's progression? The instruction to ask for wisdom (verse 5) follows the command to count pain as joy (verse 2). Wisdom only follows when you add up your experiences according to God's direction. God says, "pain adds up to the sum of joy." Want more wisdom? Count your pain as a plus. Pain instructs and helps and should be reckoned as joy. If it does, you become wiser. But if you don't count pain as joy, don't count on getting wisdom either. Wisdom does not come when you misperceive pain.

So, to get wisdom, don't just tolerate pain, but consider it a great joy. Embrace it. You'll be wiser for it.

## 6. Read the chapter in Proverbs corresponding to the day of the month.

Why read Proverbs? The whole book is dedicated to wisdom. Just as Proverbs contains thirty-one chapters, most months count thirty-one days. On the first of the month, read the first chapter of Proverbs, and so on. I've done this several times. It gets richer and deeper as I use different translations of the Bible. Here are translations to try:

**Contemporary English Version**—The CEV's writers wrote it to be read aloud. It pokes more poignantly than other versions, but it often spurs me to action. The Proverbs especially seem to ring truer in this translation.

**New Living Translation**—The modern flow blows like a breeze giving fresh perspective.

**English Standard Version**—Clear and concise, this translation continues to gain acceptance. On the spectrum between "word for word" and "thought for thought" translations, it lands in the "word for word" camp. It's a good place to be.

**New American Standard Bible**—My OT seminary professor described the NASB as "wooden but word-for-word accurate." He's right. It feels like a shot in the arm rather than a massage. But sometimes, I need the shot.

**New King James Version**—Depending on your background with Bible reading (and age, somewhat), the NKJV feels like talking to an old friend but one you understand better than its heavily accented ancestor, the KJV.

**New International Version**—Its plain talk makes sense of old things in new ways. Its clarity attaches itself to specific issues in your life while helping you address and apply wisdom to previously overlooked areas.

> *"Wisdom is more precious than rubies; nothing you desire*
> *can compare with her. She offers you long life in her right hand,*
> *and riches and honor in her left."*
> —Proverbs 3:15–16 (NLT)

## 7. Take on a new challenge.

> *"The significant challenges we face cannot be solved at the same level*
> *of thinking we were at when we created them."*
> —Albert Einstein

If you think what you've always thought, you'll do what you've always done. If you do what you've always done, you will get what you've always gotten.

Wisdom does not work in the ruts. You won't know what you don't know until you do something new. For a pastor, you might announce a sermon series on a subject you know little (or nothing) about. For any of us, you could buy a rental house or register to run a 10K or write a book. Each of these endeavors stretched my thinking. It spurred questions I didn't know to ask before committing to the actions. With new questions came new answers, which brought increased wisdom.

Jesus increased first by wisdom. How will you increase yours? Circle three of the above ways to increase the wisdom you will integrate into your life.

Jesus chose wisdom to develop Himself. It's listed first in Luke 2:52 because it's the key personal skill to all the others, even our physical bodies.

# Chapter 8

# STATURE–PHYSICAL HEALTH

*"I may die young, but I don't want it to be my fault."*
—James B. Dobbs, Esquire

We can never go beyond where our physical health can take us.

When the Apostle Paul says, "I buffet my body" (1 Corinthians 9:27, ASV), he meant he disciplined his body. He did not mean to feed it at a smorgasbord.

## My Mom's Boyfriend

Jack sat in my late dad's chair. My mom was to the right of her "boyfriend," and I was on the couch in the living room where we grew up, facing him. Jack loved the Lord and my mom, from what I could tell. He was a standup guy from all indications. But his presence still felt like a takeover, some kind of a coup d'état. It wasn't Jack's fault. My father was not there because he had died of a heart attack several months prior.

My dad's unquestioned leadership in the home "ruled the roost" all my life. At five feet, six inches tall and 425 pounds, he refused the doctor's advice for years. He seemed to rely on past athletic achievements to carry him physically. I heard him say, "No more medicine," a few times.

Dad suffered a major heart attack on Christmas Day 1999. My mom, brothers, and I made the heartrending decision to remove him from life support five weeks later. It was a terrible time for all of us. Because Dad didn't take care of himself physically, another man now sat where he sat, physically and metaphorically. Things my dad knew about life, our family's history, and his wealth of wisdom were all lost when his life ended. I still miss him. He would be so proud of my kids and now my grandkids. Unfortunately, my grandkids never met him and never got one of his bear hugs, gentle teasing, or the unconditional love I received. His death is still an unfilled hole.

We can all strive to excel mentally, spiritually, and emotionally. But if we ignore our physical health, the rest comes to a crashing halt. Now, we know ignoring our physical health affects our bodies. But it also withdraws companionship from your spouse, removes your influence from your family, and leaves a gaping hole no one else can fill. Who else will be there to support, love, and encourage your spouse, kids, grandkids, and the others in your life? Nobody will do it like you do. I've seen many widows and widowers adrift because of a lack of attention to the physical body by the deceased spouse.

On the other hand, a lot of things happen to us over which we have no control. Accidents, diseases, congenital abnormalities, and the breakdown of our bodies as we age all create physical health challenges. We cannot control those things. But we can help them in most instances by doing what we can do physically. Taking care of your physical body improves the things you can control and reduces the harmful effects of things you cannot control. Like wisdom, favor with God, and favor with people, we choose our physical pursuits.

*"Jesus grew in wisdom and stature, and in favor with God and man."*
—Luke 2:52

## The Centrality of the Physical Body for the Church

God makes a big deal out of our physical bodies. Let's not forget He uses our physical body to explain the church herself. "For just as the body is one and has many members, and all the members of the body, though many, are one body, so it is with Christ" (1 Corinthians 12:12, ESV). The Apostle Paul goes on to show the interdependence and the importance of the body working together. "The eye cannot say to the hand, 'I have no need of you'" (verse 21). Paul uses our physical bodies to explain the unity God expects from our local, spiritual bodies.

What do you call it when all the parts of the body work in unity? We call it health. When your bodily parts work the way they were designed, we say we are healthy. On the other hand, we call lack of health "disease," or dis + ease. When you are not healthy, you lack "ease." When your body maintains health, you possess an ease that is absent with illness. Walking, standing, bending, eating, and moving are all "ease + ier" when your body is in proportion and you optimally exchange carbon dioxide and oxygen. As church folks, we certainly want healthy spiritual bodies. Likewise, Christ wants healthy physical bodies. Physical health enables spiritual development in the way lack of health hinders it.

### Both ordinances focus on the physical.

Surprisingly enough, another way God shows our connection to the physical is through the ordinances of the church. Baptism and the Lord's Supper both pinpoint the importance of the corporal. Although different traditions administer the ordinances in various ways, the commonalities signal the body's significance. The Lord Jesus institutes the Lord's Supper in the Gospel of Matthew: "Now as they were eating, Jesus took bread, and after blessing it broke it and gave it to the disciples, and said, 'Take, eat; this is my body.' And he took a cup, and when he had given thanks he gave it to them, saying, 'Drink of it, all of you, for this is my blood of the covenant, which is poured out for many for the forgiveness of sins'" (Matthew 26:26–28, ESV).

Jesus used two elements: the bread and the cup. And look what he tells us about the bread: "This is my body." And what does He say about the cup? "This is my blood." Does it get any more physical than the body and the blood?

Let's look a step further, though. What is it we do when we partake of the Lord's Supper? What physical functions do we perform? We do two things. We take two actions and both are fundamentally physical. Here they are: We eat. We drink.

Look around during the Lord's Supper at your church, and you will see people physically chewing the bread. You will also notice partakers imbibing drinks from a cup: eating and drinking. Consider the significance of what God prescribes here.

For us to remember His Son, God did not just say, "Just think about Him." Don't just ruminate or ponder. Instead, God says, to really remember the sacrifice of my Son, I want you to do something, and that something is what you do every day of your life: eat and drink. I want you to perform a basic physical act to remember the spiritual. That's the Lord's Supper.

What about baptism? Depending upon your tradition, you probably follow one of three modes of baptism:

➡ Immersion: putting the person entirely under the water
➡ Aspersion: sprinkling water on the person
➡ Affusion: pouring water on the person

Notice all three methods involve water, which comprises "up to 60 percent of the human adult body."[18]

All three systems of baptism use water on the outside of the physical body. Even this use of water on our external beings encompasses physical movement. The most movement (of the three modes) occurs in immersion, where one person physically grasps the baptismal candidate and puts that person under the water. That entails a lot of physicality. Similarly, aspersion and affusion also require physical movement. These two ways necessarily include holding a person while someone pours or sprinkles water on that person. Notice all three modes include physical touch between at least two people. Baptism is fundamentally physical when you analyze the exact motions taken.

So, the Lord's Supper includes eating and drinking. Plus, baptism incorporates physical touch and water on the outside of the body. Eating, drinking, and physical movement. Compare this to taking care of our physical bodies. Most physical training designates what you eat, what you drink, and how you move (exercise). In all the hubbub of innumerable health improvement systems, two things remain constant: diet and exercise. The Lord's Supper involves diet, whereas baptism necessitates exercise.

Furthermore, the Lord's Supper permeates every part of our physical bodies internally through eating and drinking. When we eat and drink, that sustenance provides fuel and energy for every fiber of our being. Food and drink work to resource all our undertakings. It's internally complete. And, whereas the Lord's Supper touches all parts internally, the pouring or sprinkling or immersing in water covers us (or part of us) externally. The Lord's Supper physically touches us internally, and Baptism physically touches us externally. Summarily, Jesus's two ordinances for His body require a physical connection.

## God's Plan Required the Physical

God Himself thought it necessary to operate physically and not just spiritually. The All-Knowing, Ever-Present, and All-Powerful God reached the created world through the physical birth of His Son. In the sending of His Son, John 1:14 (ESV) tells us, "And the Word became flesh and dwelt among us." Flesh and bone, water and blood, Jesus came physically as we all do. God used the fundamental tactile process of human birth, common to every person, to advance His redemptive plan. He continued Jesus's mission using touch, among other things: "And Jesus stretched out his hand and touched him, saying, 'I will; be clean.' And immediately his leprosy was cleansed" (Matthew 8:3, ESV). Then God saw the achievement of the gospel plan through profound pain and suffering, resulting in physical death.

If the spiritual sufficed, Jesus could have avoided a lot of pain and agony. But the physical was required: "By sending his own Son in the likeness of sinful flesh and for sin, he condemned sin in the flesh" (Romans 8:3, ESV). Part and parcel of God's plan demanded the inclusion of the physical in the experiences shared by all: birth and death. Far from an afterthought or a look over, God worked bodily in redemption.

## The Process of Becoming Like Christ Includes the Physical

At the onset of our salvation, Christ's work begins forming us into Himself. This shift from spiritual death to spiritual life occurs instantaneously. Sometimes called justification, Christ redeems and alters our spirit. "And those whom he called he also justified" (Romans 8:30, ESV).

After justification, we yield ourselves to Christ's guidance through a process of sanctification. The word "Sanctus" means "holy." We embark on a journey of becoming more like Jesus. Whereas justification changes the spirit within us, sanctification endeavors to adjust our soul. Our personality and proclivities undergo a spiritual construction to reshape us, to reform us into the image of Christ. But even this soul-shaping includes the physical: "For this is the will of God, your sanctification: that you abstain from sexual immorality; that each one of you know how to control his own body in holiness and honor" (1 Thessalonians 4:3–4, ESV).

There is yet a third phase of our becoming like Christ: glorification. This glorification forever alters our physical bodies, so they, too, emulate Christ Himself.

You and your physical health sit center stage in God's plan to develop you. He gave you a malleable tool to escalate His work through you. Your physical health, even with pre-existing and some uncontrollable conditions, depends squarely on you.

To help you move forward, list two behaviors that would increase you physically:

1.
2.

# How to Increase Yourself Physically

Increasing in stature (improving physically) comes in two primary forms: eat well and strengthen your body (which includes exercise and rest).

Remember:

→ Every bit of portioned healthy food you put in your body makes it function better.
→ Every time you exercise, you get stronger.
→ Every time you walk/run/do cardio, you get healthier.

Every time you eat the wrong food or too much of the right food or miss strength training or cardio, you miss an opportunity to get stronger and healthier.

## Eat Healthy Food in Proper Portions

Our bodies can only use the fuel we give them. Doing a quick search of recommended eating shows that we should avoid certain foods and focus on consuming healthy things. I am not a nutritionist, but reading to learn about what's good, what's okay, and what's not-so-good to feed my body guides me every day. It will do the same for you.

Numerous programs exist to guide us in eating better. If you want to reduce your overall weight, any diet will work if you work it. Every diet plan I have seen shows "before and after" pictures. Each plan worked for somebody. It worked for a body that followed the plan. (I [too often] tell the joke: "I emailed my before and after pictures to the website. The site put both pictures in the 'before' column!")

If you "kind of work the program" or do a "variation of XYZ program," it won't work because you are not working the program. Find a singular healthy eating plan and follow it totally. In the days I was "kind of following" a certain plan, my weight did not improve. I didn't lose weight because "kind of following the plan" meant I did not follow the plan. I failed to track my food consumption before eating it, which meant I did not record what I ate.

Then I came across this insightful advice: "Don't guess and don't estimate." Record exactly what you eat just before you eat it. If you eat first, then track it, it's an estimate. I have found what looks deceptively like one cup of cereal in the bowl turns out to be two and a half cups when you measure it. As it turns out, any amount of guessing or estimating means you are not following the plan. When I say, "The program does not work for me," what I really mean is, "I am not working the program."

## Two Misconceptions About Losing Weight

1. "If I work out more, I can eat more and still lose weight." So I ate more. And I gained weight. Oops. That is not what I had in mind.
2. "If I work out more and eat the same amount, I can lose weight."

That did not work either. It's rather anecdotal, but it seems to be true: "Losing weight is 80 percent dependent on what you eat." That means working out, while good for us, won't help us lose significant weight.

## Exercise

Increasing the resistance to your body's movement strengthens your muscles and bones. Pushing your body against added weight, either weight you lift or the weight of your own body, increases your physical resilience.

As an added positive by-product, pushing your body physically also increases the resilience of your mind. The mental shift you make between "I don't think I can do it" and "I did it!" also aids your increase mentally, spiritually, and emotionally. We choose our views, and then our views shape us. Conversely, physically quitting fires off the "quit instinct" mentally, spiritually, and emotionally. Our chosen views in one area of our lives show up in other areas of our lives, even in places we don't expect.

---

### We choose our views, and then our views shape us.

---

Eat healthy, portioned food and push your body physically three to five times a week. You will be healthier. The routine will also help buoy your improvement mentally, spiritually, and emotionally.

Increasing in stature means you give attention to your physical body. Objectively, here are some helpful measures:

- Blood glucose levels
- Amount of cholesterol (both good and bad)
- VO2 max levels
- Mileage pace
- Percentage of body fat
- Resting heart rate
- BMI (Body Mass Index)
- Weight
- Vision
- Personal grooming (haircut, facial hair)
- Condition of our teeth and gums
- Personal hygiene

As these indicators improve, your physical body gets better. Your body's health affects you and affects others in your effectiveness for Christ. Jesus increased in stature. Let us do likewise.

*Chapter 9*

# FAVOR WITH GOD
# –SPIRITUAL CONNECTION

*"Remember me, O Lord, when you show favor to your people;*
*help me when you save them."*
—Psalm 106:4 (ESV)

## Personal Surrender

*"Put God first. Put God first in everything you do."*
—Denzel Washington, Commencement address at Dillard University

As a twenty-six-year-old pastor of a church that had been in decline for twenty-five years, I didn't know what I didn't know. Although reared in church and seminary-trained, the fundamental process of personal surrender eluded me. I discovered it in my first two weeks at that first church.

Seeing the church's quarter-century declining statistics marked the beginning of a downward spiral in my self-appraisal as well as all I thought I knew. In all the difficulty of that first church (which I refer to as my "dark night of the soul"), God imprinted a concept into the heart of my soul that I must never forget. I've rediscovered its truth at every major advancement of kingdom work.

I have come to believe I must surrender myself at deeper levels for God to do greater works through me and the ministries I lead.

God requires more surrender at each juncture, it seems. I hesitate to call surrender a spiritual discipline because surrender is not what I do; it's often what I cease doing. Sometimes surrender shows up as what I need to stop believing. I don't acquire surrender. Surrender requires a release. But unlike the spiritual disciplines, the release differs every time. In surrender, God mashes another part of me, so my beliefs or passions or attitudes (or anything else, God must access it all) must be newly yielded to Him.

Sometimes the surrender demands a deeper relinquishment of a former issue. Sometimes surrender knocks on a new door in my heart. What I do know is every time God moves to do greater work through me, He requires an increased yielding in me. He required a surrender from Moses as Moses relinquished his reticence to speak publicly. God overcame Joseph's hesitation as his betrothed gave birth to the Savior. Maybe most notable, God required it of His Son. See the picture of perfect surrender from the lips of Jesus in the Garden of Gethsemane before His crucifixion: "Abba, Father," he cried out, "everything is possible for you. Please take this cup of suffering away from me. Yet I want your will to be done, not mine" (Mark 14:36, NLT).

Enjoying God's favor requires a surrender of anything God desires to remove from us or add to us. Spiritual disciplines show us additional ways to align our lives to Him.

## Spiritual Disciplines

> *"But seek first the kingdom of God and his righteousness, and all these*
> *things will be added to you."*
> —Matthew 6:33 (ESV)

Seeking God's favor should remain at the forefront of our hearts and minds each day. Here are twelve spiritual disciplines to help us seek and obtain favor from the Lord:

## 1. Whisper and the Word (Daily Quiet Time)

The Bible tells us God did not speak to Elijah in the wind, not in the earthquake, and not in the fire. God spoke in a *"still, small voice"* (1 Kings 19, NKJV). You only hear a small voice when everything around you is quiet. The quietest moments in many homes only happen in the mornings, alone, when you listen.

## 2. Journaling

Pen in hand, my pad opens to the blank page for that day. I write my prayers to God and tell Him anything I am thinking. Years ago, I gave up closing my eyes and talking to Him. My mind runs like an escaped convict when I do that, and I rarely return to the task at hand, which includes praying. Writing forces my focus and feels connected. The neurological pressure from my fingertips through the pen onto the page fires my synapses in reinforcing ways. I think more clearly when I write and express a depth to the God of My Redemption. I have found few other ways. The biblical book of Lamentations is the prayer journal of Jeremiah. The book of Psalms is the prayer journal of David. It's a great model for us to follow.

## 3. Fasting

Going without food focuses my attention on the transcendent. I love food. Its taste carries one of the great pleasures of life. It's fun to shop for it, find it, cook it, slow smoke it on my barbecue smoker, and fire it on the grill. I LOVE food and eating. Intentionally setting it aside for a day each month, as I have done for years, shows God that I love Him more. Matthew 6:16 shows me God expects it: "When you fast . . ."

## 4. Solitude

Sit for thirty minutes and absolve your mind of all but what God wants to tell you. The earliest minutes provide the biggest struggle, which helps prove why it's important. You do not control your life or those around you when you sit silently. Although it seems like God takes over during that time, what you realize is He takes over all the time. It's always true. The value comes in your realization.

## 5. Prayer

Talking to God throughout the day keeps you connected to Him. I write in the morning to discover His direction for the day. Yet things happen that I can't foresee. Maintaining my dialogue with Him throughout my waking hours clears my thinking, calibrates my reactions, and provides a valued connection with my most trusted Confidant. Ending the day praying with your spouse opens your mind to even hear from the Lord while your eyes are closed. "I will bless the Lord who guides me; even at night my heart instructs me" (Psalm 16:7, NLT).

## 6. Simplicity

Choose one instead of many. Many options unnecessarily clutter the mind. Some argue many choices result in decision fatigue. Every decision you make means one less decision you can make effectively. Why use your mental agility with things that are perishing when your focus could be the kingdom of Christ?

## 7. Sabbath

Take one day each week when you don't think, talk, or read about work from the time you wake up until the time you go to bed. This is hardest for pastors. Don't mistake the ministry for the Master. Those are two different things. Your work at, and with, the church is absolutely work. Sunday is not your Sabbath. Pick another day, every week.

Since the God of All Creation thought it best to take a day off each week, why would I think I don't need it? And why would you take a Sabbath? You may not feel the need to rest physically, but you need the distance from the work to gain a fuller perspective. When your nose is against the grindstone, you cannot see the larger patterns at play. Adjusting those patterns will produce far more fruit than slight adjustments to the stone.

## 8. Meditation

Choose one Bible verse for a week and ask God to show you its implications in your life.

Reading Bible verses grants an overall perspective and a sense of the trajectory of God's work. Narrowing your focus to one verse pushes that truth into you for the rest of your life: even popular verses, like Psalm 23:1, yield precious treasure when we marinate in it.

## 9. Bible Study

Read a passage of Scripture and ask yourself four questions:

1. What does it say? (Observation)
2. What does it mean? (Interpretation)
3. What else does the Bible say about this? (Correlation)
4. What does this mean to me? (Application)

A way to remember these four questions is to say, Oh (observation) I (interpretation) See ("C," correlation) A (application) way to understand the Bible. Devotional reading only dips so deep. Mining the truths of the Scriptures unearths the most valued nuggets.

## 10. Stewardship

As reported, Jesus said more about money than He did heaven, hell, prayer, and faith combined. One of every ten verses in the four gospels deals with money or the use of possessions. Sixteen of Jesus's thirty-eight parables focus on the fiscal. God says things about money that He does not say about anything else. He tells us the state of your finances reflects the condition of your heart. "For where your treasure is, there your heart will be also" (Matthew 6:21). For example, if you are in inordinate debt, it pulls too much of your heart's attention. Stress and anxiety come from a lack of financial management, which is why stewardship is a spiritual discipline. Effectively stewarding your money unshackles your heart and frees your soul. Lack of financial acumen restrains your spiritual development according to Luke 16:11 (ESV): "If then you have not been faithful in the unrighteous wealth, who will entrust to you the true riches?" When you properly manage your money, you increase your favor with God.

---

The state of your finances reflects the condition of your heart.

---

## 11. Secrecy

"Beware of practicing your righteousness before other people in order to be seen by them, for then you will have no reward from your Father who is in heaven," the Bible tells us in Matthew 6:1 (ESV). What praiseworthy action do you perform that only God knows? Everything good does not need to be done in secret. But honoring God means some beautiful actions should lack a broadcast.

## 12. Serving

We serve when we do nice things for other people. If you are a minister, you spend most of your waking hours serving. Your preaching, teaching, counseling, and encouraging all fulfill this spiritual discipline. A common error for pastors is to think you aren't doing enough. A good friend asked me at lunch, "What do you think you need to be doing?" I said, "Serving other people." He wisely said, "You're already doing that. What else do you want to do?" If you do serve others, it's a spiritual discipline. If you think you aren't doing enough, you might check with someone who knows you to get a different perspective. If you lead in an organization and your leading doesn't include serving others, it's a great discipline to embrace.

## Take Four Steps to Increase Your Favor with God

1. Identify the spiritual disciplines on the next page that you exercise regularly. Draw a circle around them.
2. Put a rectangle around the disciplines you haven't considered until now.
3. Star (*) the spiritual disciplines you have reasons for not following.
4. Adopt one of the spiritual disciplines you have a reason for not following (in addition to following the ones you consistently follow). If your desire to deepen spiritually exceeds your explanations, you will find a more connected soul on the other side of your hesitation. Test it.

# SPIRITUAL DISCIPLINES

| DAILY QUIET TIME | JOURNALING | FASTING |
|---|---|---|
| Taking time each day to talk and listen to God | Spending time writing my thoughts to God | Going without food or something meaningful for 24 hours |

| SOLITUDE | PRAYER | SIMPLICITY |
|---|---|---|
| Sitting for 30 minutes without distraction | Talking to God | Choosing one instead of many |

| SABBATH | MEDITATION | BIBLE STUDY |
|---|---|---|
| Having one day each week when you don't think about, read about, or do work from the time you wake up until you go to bed | Choosing one Bible verse and asking God to show you its implications in your life | Read a passage of Scripture and ask 4 questions: 1. What does it say? 2. What does it mean? 3. What else does the Bible say about this? 4. What does this mean to me? |

| STEWARDSHIP | SECRECY | SERVING |
|---|---|---|
| Giving the first 10% of my income to God | Doing or accomplishing something and only telling God about it | Performing a physical act of kindness to another person |

## Chapter 10

# FAVOR WITH PEOPLE –EMOTIONAL DEPTH

## Oversized Casket

*"And this is my prayer: that your love may abound*
*more and more in knowledge and depth of insight."*
—Philippians 1:9

Nestled in the Eastern Kentucky hills stands a statue of Keith Whitley. He isn't buried in that Sandy Hook cemetery, but he's from there. His birthplace, coupled with his rise through the ranks of country music, merits the remembrance.

The burial of a retired army veteran formed the occasion. The veteran's fourth wife (some thought fifth), a Mormon from Germany in her twenties with limited English skills, stood nearby. The funeral director conscripted the pallbearers to lower the body into the earth. A funeral home or cemetery employee typically performs the service. I don't know why none were there. Nevertheless, the dressed-up pallbearers complied with the director's wishes.

Long ago, the deceased army veteran lost his military service physique, necessitating an oversized casket. The funeral home got that right. What they missed, however, was that an oversized casket requires an oversized hole. This became apparent as the pallbearers lowered the heavier than usual casket into the not-quite-big-enough opening in the earth. It didn't fit. It got stuck near the midway point to its final destination.

Not wanting to delay the interment (maybe because he didn't have anyone to help if the pallbearers left), the funeral director forced the issue by trying to force the body into its resting place. With the casket stuck about halfway down the hole, the funeral director commenced stomping on the casket to get it to go down.

Stomp! Like an angry baseball player called out at home plate. Stomp! While hanging onto somebody's arm so he wouldn't fall into the hole, Stomp! Stomp! Stomp!

Glances went to the horrified widow as the director pounded the casket of her deceased husband with his foot!

What a way to go!

That funeral director lacked what all leaders need: interpersonal skills. He may have gotten the casket to the required depth. But he had little insight or understanding of how shocked and disturbed other people would feel by his method.

Leaders earn favor with people when they understand what others are thinking and feeling by reading their words, tone, body language, and actions. Great leaders understand, study, and relate well to other people. They hold a social awareness of their current situation and ably read the nonverbal signals constantly in play.

***Good leaders read the lines. Great leaders read between the lines.***

The *Portland Business Journal* describes interpersonal skills like this: "Perhaps a more helpful way to describe this skill set is to note several of the typical characteristics of individuals who possess effective people skills:

→ They understand themselves and how their behavior impacts others.
→ They control their responses; they try to be less impulsive and think before acting.
→ They have a sincere desire to assist others in the pursuit of goals.
→ They are able to 'tune in' accurately to the feelings and needs of others and then treat people accordingly.

→ They work at managing relationships, building networks, and finding common ground to minimize conflict and maximize rapport.

→ They are consistently approachable.

→ They create an environment of trust."[19]

Notice interpersonal skills don't only include understanding other people. Favor with others includes recognizing and managing your own emotional state because your internal emotional condition directly impacts your favor with others.

*"93 percent of our communication is nonverbal."*
—Albert Mehrabian

You cannot control others. But you can control your own emotional state, which directly influences others. Nothing else affects your relationships as much. Leaders sometimes hesitate because of fear or lack of confidence. Emotions can cause us to think more or research more rather than act.

Conversely, the same emotions inside a leader can ignite an explosion creating collateral damage in the hearts of others. Both the hesitation and the explosion severely limit your impact and effectiveness. To increase in favor with others, avoid both.

Typically, the leader inherently knows what to do. Rarely does a leader *not* have an idea about what direction to take. Sometimes it takes a while, but leaders lead. Unfortunately, because of a lack of certainty (an emotional lack), the doing does not get done. Emotional hurdles prevent good leaders from becoming great leaders.

Great leadership requires managing the angst and anxiety of your own internal world. For many leaders and me, the greatest leadership challenge is emotional, which is why favor with others plays a key role in guiding a group of people. When we succumb to ourselves, we question ourselves:

→ What if this initiative bombs?

→ When will they find out I don't know what I'm doing? (Imposter Syndrome)

→ I'm not sure this is the right direction to pursue, so I won't move forward with it.

→ I will move forward with the initiative, but I won't tell anyone. Because if I don't tell anyone and it fails, then I won't be seen as a failure. (By the way, not telling anyone about a new initiative almost guarantees it won't go well.)

On the other hand, when we yield our internal worlds to trust in God, we move forward once we gain clarity. I know leaders struggle with these same questions. The difference between great leaders and everybody else is great leaders go ahead and make the move. They act in spite of the internal questioning. The difference between fear and courage is courage does what was feared.

Great leaders build favor with other people. But how do they do it? What are key behaviors to help you increase your interpersonal skills?

*"Often the difference between a successful man and a failure is not one's better abilities or ideas, but the courage that one has to bet on his ideas, to take a calculated risk, and to act."*
—Maxwell Maltz

## The Golden Rule

*"The ability to deal with people is as purchasable a commodity as sugar or coffee, and I will pay more for that ability than for any other under the sun."*
—John D. Rockefeller

### Indications That You Need to Increase Favor with People

All great leaders agree it's important to get along well with people. We feel others' interpersonal skills or lack of them. It's harder to figure out where we stand. Here are some possible indicators you need to increase your favor with others:

→ You see people flinch when you are talking.
→ You find yourself saying or thinking, "They took that the wrong way!"
→ You use the phrase "Just kidding!"

→ You tell people what's on your mind.

→ Friendships erode and you don't seem to know why.

→ In a conversation, you do most of the talking.

→ You tell people nice things that aren't true.

## The Golden Rule Provides a Path to Increase Our Favor with Others

All these indicators of people who lack favor with others can be avoided. One way to remedy these behaviors is to follow Jesus's instruction in the gospel of Matthew. You can increase favor with people by following the Golden Rule. In the Sermon on the Mount (Matthew 5–7), Jesus gives us a picture of the expected behavior for His followers. After giving several examples of how to treat others, He summarizes our relationships with others like this: "In everything, therefore, treat people the same way you want them to treat you, for this is the Law and the Prophets" (Matthew 7:12, NASB).

The Contemporary English Version (which was written to be read aloud) says: "Treat others as you want them to treat you. This is what the Law and the Prophets are all about" (Matthew 7:12, CEV).

Jesus gave us a comprehensive picture of how to increase in favor with people. He used this summation to encapsulate all of Scripture ("Law and the Prophets") as it existed in His day. Note a couple of things about this principle:

**It's personal.** Base your actions toward others on how you—yes, you, in particular—want others to treat you. What attitudes do you desire from others? How do you like to be approached? Use your drives to drive your behavior and disposition toward others.

**It initiates.** Often the Golden Rule gets misinterpreted as something like, "I don't want people lying to me so that I won't lie to others." But that's not what this says. To follow the Golden Rule and increase your favor with others, you need to initiate. You go first. You introduce to another person what you would want that person to do for you. "Treat people . . ." states a positive action, not a reaction.

Here's a way this could work when you see a person standing in a room of people: "If I were in that person's shoes, I would like somebody to come over and talk to me." Then, you go talk to that person. Don't wait. Increasing favor with others includes proactively doing, not waiting, and responding. How do we know what people want?

## What Every Person Wants

- → To be valued
- → To be heard
- → To be supported
- → To believe the best about me
- → To remember my name
- → To be nice to me even if I'm not nice to you
- → To bring me a glass of iced tea on a hot summer day

Treating people the way you want to be treated goes a long way toward building your emotional capacity. Resolving conflict also builds emotional capacity in you and in the organization you lead.

# Conflict Resolution

Matthew 5:9 (ESV) ascribes a blessing to those who resolve conflict. "Blessed are the peacemakers, for they shall be called sons of God." God does not bless people who maintain the peace, who don't ruffle feathers. It's not the "peacekeepers" who will be called sons of God. The "peacemakers" get the title. Blessed are those who walk into turbulent situations and create peace. Creating peace requires emotional capacity, a "favor with others" that does not occur naturally. But you can develop it.

Interestingly, the first two mentions of "church" in the Bible include conflict. Matthew 16:18 first lists the word, and a quick five verses later, conflict appears. "Get behind me, Satan!" Jesus said to one of His closest allies in verse 23. Jesus instituted the church in Matthew 16, shared the plan, then conflict broke out. Sound familiar?

The second time "church" appears (Matthew 18:17), the whole passage focuses on how to resolve conflict. So why would a pastor think conflict can or should be avoided? Pastors I know tend to avoid conflict for a variety of reasons. Perhaps you can see yourself in one of these. (I know I can see me.):

→ They don't feel confident in their ability to deal with conflict.

→ They fear "blowing up" and doing more damage than what already exists.

→ They don't think they can handle the personal anxiety it would take to address the conflict.

→ They do not feel like they can live with the personal anxiety between the time the problem/conflict is addressed and it is resolved.

→ They hope the problem will be resolved without their connection to it.

→ They do not want people to be unhappy with them.

→ They are afraid the person(s) involved will leave the church.

→ They fear what other people in the church may do or say because the leader addressed the problem/conflict.

This seems like a pretty disjointed list. But it really centers on one particular area. Do you see it? Do you notice any similarities among the list here? Did you see any threads of meaning carried through each one? If you recognized that "they all are emotional," you are correct.

In personally dealing with conflict, coaching leaders in conflict, mediating conflict in small groups (often with the pastor at the table), or managing conflict for an entire church, the emotional component of conflict is the primary challenge of dealing with it. The good news is that resolving conflict is an entirely learnable skill. No matter your background or disposition, you can learn how to bring conflicted people together. Even better, the more you grow in your ability to handle conflict, the less you will have to deal with it in your church. Once people realize conflict will be resolved, they are less likely to create problems. The additional bonus to learning how to deal with conflict is that its emotional drain on you goes down dramatically.

Talk to most any church leader and ask, "How should you handle the conflict?" and the answer will be, "Go talk to the person." Then pastors typically cite Matthew 18:15 (ESV): "If your brother sins against you, go and tell him his fault, between you and him alone." Good step. It's really the best first step. Do not try to settle it on the phone. Don't email. Do not reply to their email with an email. Refuse to text or send a letter. Go physically and talk to the person or have them meet you personally, face-to-face in your office. Depending on the situation, sometimes you should have somebody else with you when you meet personally. So why don't leaders meet with the people and resolve it? From what pastors tell me, they lack the emotional capacity to do it. They know what to do. They just "can't bring themselves" to meet with the conflicted parties and bring them to resolution.

A panicked pastor called me. He briefly explained the conflict between two families in his church. "I just went to see the first family. I'm on my way to visit the other family (in the conflict). What should I do?" I told him, "Don't go." He then said, "Well, what should I do then?" "Get both families in your office at the same time and work it out." He said, "That would probably create a lot of tension." Exactly. And that's part of the process for resolving conflict. What helps resolve any conflict is getting both parties in the same space. When mediated well, those tensions between the two parties work to level themselves in both parties. It's really a beautiful thing. It does take emotional energy, but it's the only way to resolve a problem.

On the other hand, if you deal with the parties separately, all that anxiety lands on you. I think that's why many leaders avoid conflict. They think they have to carry the angst. Let me free you from that assumption.

Now, no good leader likes conflict. A few leaders constantly look for a fight, but they don't last in the ministry. Effective leaders deal with their emotional stuff to successfully learn and lead through discordance. Learning how to effectively maneuver parties at odds with each other to unity requires a leader who is growing in favor with others. The good news is you can learn how. It's as much an emotional skill as it is mental, but you can do it.

Leadership necessitates certain knowledge. But it's rarely a lack of knowledge that limits leaders. It's the emotional stuff that stunts leaders' growth. Emotional learning poses a much steeper climb for most of us. If you are willing to allow God to change you, you can excel in this area. Some people seem to have an edge if they grew up in a healthy environment. But I've seen pastors who excelled in favor with people who come from severely dysfunctional upbringings. So, pastor, no matter your background and context, you can get there. Peace and joy await you on the other side of dealing with conflict.

Just as Jesus increased in "favor with others," we can, too. So, how can we grow emotionally? What sort of process or principles should we follow to increase in favor with others?

One way is to identify where we go on tilt emotionally. What sets us off is an indication of where we need work. "I only get out of sorts when people don't put their dishes in the sink after dinner," shows an emotional flashpoint. I then ask myself, "Why do dishes set me off?" Raising the issue with yourself begins the learning. Learning to modulate my internal state in those situations shows I'm growing in my emotional capacity and my favor with others.

Here are a few other potential indicators:

→ What hijacks your day?
→ When do you scream or yell?
→ What activities (and by whom) make you withdraw into your shell and not interact with people?
→ What happens right before your spouse and children avoid you at home?
→ What sets you off?

One of the best definitions I have seen of emotional maturity is: "The ability to go against your natural bent (inclinations) when under pressure."

As you have seen in life, some people act like skunks when under pressure, and some perform like turtles. When a skunk is pressured, everybody knows! If a skunk gets rattled, he sprays everybody and everything around him!

Conversely, when turtles feel attacked, they go inside their shell. If you yell at a turtle, they just stay in the shell longer. So what does emotional maturity look like for a skunk? An emotionally mature skunk will hold the spray when threatened. And a turtle? A turtle who has favor with people will stick their neck out, even when feeling anxious.

## Why Do I Need to Increase My Emotional Capacity?

But why? Why would a leader go down the difficult road of exploring and increasing their emotional capacity? Why can I just not go with what I have? Many believe that. Then they wonder why things do not go well.

*If you do not recognize (and resolve) your emotional pitfalls, you won't recognize them in others.*

**The lack of recognition of emerging problems can wreck a church.**

Dr. Bill Agee has equipped hundreds of church planters around the world. He taught me this truth: "Problems early are hard to see but easy to solve. Problems later are easy to see but hard to resolve."

The way to recognize problems early is to have enough emotional maturity to see what's happening. Leaders who do not recognize their own internal conflict don't see it coming organizationally until it's too late to resolve easily. Leaders who do not learn how to manage their own internal state don't see problems until they blow up.

On the other hand, emotionally mature leaders see problems early. They intervene before conflicts get bigger. A leader with a strong emotional constitution solves problems before most of your congregation even knows there is a problem. That's the kind of leader God uses greatly.

As we have seen, Jesus operated a personal strategy. He gained clarity on His personal mission. Then, from age twelve, He increased in wisdom (mentally), stature (physically), favor with God (spiritually), and favor with people (emotionally). These crucial personal skills form the foundation of what all of us as leaders should do and be.

Unfortunately, too many leaders stop here. But Jesus did not call a halt with a personal strategy. Instead, He launched an organizational strategy to fulfill His personal mission "to seek and to save that which was lost." His organizational strategy included starting an organization from scratch. He built the church from the ground up. In whatever organization you lead, Jesus passed that baton to you.

*Chapter 11*

# JESUS'S ORGANIZATIONAL STRATEGY–MATTHEW 16:13-23

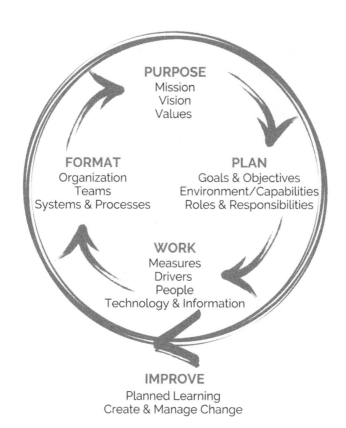

**PURPOSE**
Mission
Vision
Values

**PLAN**
Goals & Objectives
Environment/Capabilities
Roles & Responsibilities

**WORK**
Measures
Drivers
People
Technology & Information

**FORMAT**
Organization
Teams
Systems & Processes

**IMPROVE**
Planned Learning
Create & Manage Change

*"Jesus said, "I will build my church."*
—Matthew 16:18

*"One who lacks executive ability to any considerable degree, however clearly*
*he may see things spiritual, will be unable to translate his vision into action.*
*It is true that subtle dangers lie in overmuch organization, for it can be*
*a very unsatisfactory substitute for the presence and working of the Holy*
*Spirit. But that is not necessarily so. Lack of method and organization has its*
*dangers too and has spelled failure for many a promising venture for God."*
J. Oswald Sanders, *Spiritual Leadership*

## Jesus Used Organizational Principles

**J**esus possessed a clear, personal mission. He came to "seek and to save that which was lost" (Luke 19:10, NKJV). From His personal mission, He developed personal skills in ministry. Luke 2:52 tells us He "grew in wisdom and stature, and in favor with God and man." Jesus invested time to better Himself mentally, physically, spiritually, and emotionally. This tells us the greatest leader who ever lived, who developed the largest organization on the planet, spent energy bettering His personal attributes. But Jesus also focused on developing an organization, the church.

Like Jesus, church leaders need organizational skills to effectively lead a church. To be a leader like Jesus, you must identify and increase your personal skills. But to be a leader like Jesus, you must also craft your skills in leading and developing an organization.

---

### Jesus came to build an organization.

---

In Matthew 16:18, Jesus said, "And I tell you that you are Peter, and on this rock, I will build my church." Many debate what Jesus meant by "rock." But nobody argues whether or not Jesus came to build His church. So, our churches should function like we are building. This is true even when some say, "Jesus builds the church. We don't build anything." What? If that's true, why would Jesus tell His key leaders He was going to build a church? Furthermore, why does Galatians 2:9 call three of them "pillars" (Peter, James, and John)?

You build on pillars. When you build, you plan, you allocate resources, you check on progress weekly with the architect and the superintendent. You monitor progress against the blueprint, the plan for the building. Sounds like a great regimen for building the body of Christ.

As church leaders, God calls us to assist God in building the church. The Apostle Paul saw it this way: "By the grace God has given me, I laid a foundation as a wise builder, and someone else is building on it. But each one should build with care. For no one can lay any foundation other than the one already laid, which is Jesus Christ" (1 Corinthians 3:10–11). Jesus is the foundation, and we build on it. Again in 1 Corinthians 14:12, the Bible tells us to build: "Since you are eager for gifts of the Spirit, try to excel in those that build up the church." Ephesians 4:29 tells us to only do "what is helpful for building others up according to their needs, that it may benefit those who listen."

It's an all-too-common mistake to approach the organization of the church as if it's just a furtherance of our personal walk with God. It is "a furtherance," mind you, but not "just a furtherance." Most definitely, you must lead yourself. Following Christ personally forms the foundation of our leadership. But personal following alone does not build the rest of the organization. To lead a church effectively, you must acquire additional skills beyond your own personal walk with Christ.

## Here is a sampling of what Jesus did to lead the church as an organization.

**Clarify the Mission.** "The Son of Man came to seek and to save that which was lost" (Luke 19:10, ASV).

**Cast the Vision.** "I will build my church" (Matthew 16:18) and "Then the sign of the Son of Man will appear in the sky, and then all the peoples of the earth will mourn; and they will see the Son of Man coming on the clouds of heaven with power and great glory" (Matthew 24:30, CSB).

**Determine What They Should Not Do.** "For God did not send his Son into the world to condemn the world, but to save the world through him" (John 3:17).

**Correct the Behavior of Other People.** "But turning around and looking at his disciples, he rebuked Peter and said, 'Get behind me, Satan! You are not thinking about God's concerns but human concerns' (Mark 8:33, CSB).

**Direct the Behavior of Other People.** "You give them something to eat" (Mark 6:37) and "He commanded the crowd to sit down on the ground" (Mark 8:6, CSB). Some pastors and church leaders refrain from giving clear behavioral direction to people. Jesus directed people's behavior.

**Delegate Work.** Raising of Lazarus from the dead. Jesus told the people with him to "remove the stone" (John 11:39, NASB) and "Unwrap him and let him go" (John 11:44, CSB). Jesus could have performed these functions. He didn't. He delegated these tasks to others.

**Develop Leaders by Testing Them.** "So when Jesus looked up and noticed a huge crowd coming toward him, he asked Philip, 'Where will we buy bread so that these people can eat?' He asked this to test him, for he himself knew what he was going to do" (John 6:5–6, CSB).

**Develop Leaders by Giving Them Responsibility.** "After this, the Lord appointed seventy-two others, and he sent them ahead of him in pairs to every town and place where he himself was about to go" (Luke 10:1, CSB).

**Teach to Align Belief and Behavior with the Mission.** "Then he began to teach them . . ." Jesus taught the Sermon on the Mount, beginning in Matthew 5:2 (CSB).

**Model Desirable Behavior.** "Truly I tell you, the one who believes in me will also do the works that I do. And he will do even greater works than these, because I am going to the Father" (John 14:12, CSB).

**Recruit Leaders.** "'Follow me,' He told them, 'and I will make you fish for people!'" (Matthew 4:19, CSB). Jesus recruited them to be leaders who will accomplish a task.

**Time the Elements of Your Plan.** "My hour has not yet come" (John 2:4). See also John 7:6; Matthew 26:18; Mark 1:15.

**Manage Conflict.** "They came to Capernaum. When he was in the house, he asked them, 'What were you arguing about on the road?'" (Mark 9:33).

**Build an Organizational Format.** In the four lists of the twelve apostles, Jesus used an Inner Circle (Peter, James, and John), and He had three additional leadership positions within the twelve (Peter, Philip, and James of Alphaeus).

**Pay the Bills.** Jesus directed Peter to pay the temple tax (Matthew 17:24–27).

**Clarify the Organization's Values.** "You have heard that it was said . . . But I say to . . ." Matthew 5:21–22, 27–28, 33–34, 38–39, 43–44 in the Sermon on the Mount.

**Work to Increase the Impact of the Organization**. "Go out into the highways and hedges, and compel them to come in" (Luke 14:23, NKJV).

**Measure results.** Parable of the Talents (Matthew 25:14–30, ESV).

As leaders, each of us should acquire these skills. Unlike a "strengths versus weaknesses" list where we can only focus on our strengths, this list comprises a core competency for any leader. It's worth investing in yourself by growing your competency in each of these areas.

The good news is that you can learn these skills. I know I did. I grew up in a home where I didn't know people who led organizations. My mom and dad loved the Lord and taught in our local church but didn't lead organizations. I went into the ministry thinking I could just do the personal things and the church would take care of herself. My ministry life suffered before I learned I needed organizational skills. My ministry effectiveness increased dramatically once I learned and practiced strategic skills. I pray the same for you. If applied, the following sections can increase your ministry's effectiveness.

## Your Personal Calling

*"I will give you the keys to the kingdom of heaven,*
*and God in heaven will allow whatever you allow on earth.*
*But he will not allow anything you don't allow."*
—Matthew 16:19 (CEV)

Remember, Jesus started the church as a delivery system for His personal mission. For a pastor, it's vitally important that you see the church as the fulfillment of your personal mission. It's not just a job. Leading a local congregation requires a calling from God Almighty. But the truth is, every person has a calling from God. God put a personal mission inside you, business leader or nonprofit leader. Jesus knew and operated every day according to His personal mission. Do you know yours?

Without a clear sense of call, it will be difficult to do what needs to be done to increase your organization's effectiveness.

Even when you know God calls you, it's tough to get things moving in the right direction. Even with a call, there are days you want to quit your job or quit the ministry and go and do something else. Jesus built the church because He was called to "seek and to save the lost." Your clear sense of God's call will help sustain you through the tough times. The good news is when you do have a sense of God's call, and things do head in the right direction, life gets incredibly wonderful. It's worth all that it takes to get there. Your days are brighter, and the kingdom impact greater. When you start seeing the results of God's hand at work in your life and ministry, you live the life God called you to live. I would not trade it for anything. After thirty years in the ministry in varying roles, I can tell you it's worth it.

So you know God called you and you are doing what He wants you to do. The hovering question is, "How do I accomplish God's call through an organization?" In the following chapters of *The Leadership Strategy of Jesus*, you will see how all these skills Jesus used fit together and how you can implement them in your church.

*Chapter 12*

# ORGANIZATIONAL PURPOSE (MISSION, VISION, VALUES)

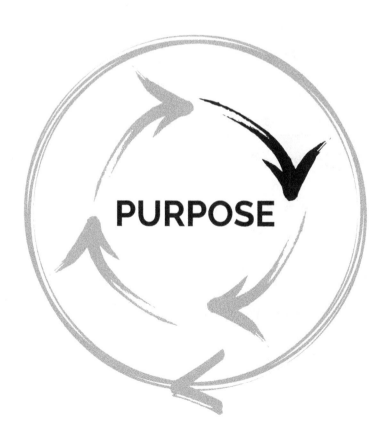

*"Would you tell me, please, which way I ought to go from here?"*
*"That depends a good deal on where you want to get to," said the Cat.*
*"I don't much care where." said Alice.*
*"Then it doesn't matter which way you go." said the Cat.*
—Lewis Carroll, *Alice in Wonderland*

E very church believes they know why they exist until you ask them.

"We are here to make disciples" is a common answer.

"How many did you make last year?" comes the question.

"I don't know."

"What is a disciple?"

Then you get a rather long answer that shows it's not clear to the pastor. When it's fuzzy in the pulpit, it's bewildering in the pews.

*"The Lord has made everything for its purpose."*
—Proverbs 16:4 (ESV)

---

Each church has a purpose, just as each child has a name.

---

# Church (Or Organization) Renewal in a Sentence

Here's a simple recipe to revolutionize your church or organization:

**"Clarify your church's/organization's compelling purpose
and realign your organization to fulfill it."**

In a nutshell, this is the job of the organizational leader. There are a lot of parts and pieces and different ways to understand and implement them, but it all comes back to your clear purpose and the actions you take to ensure it happens. Note that the purpose must also be "compelling." To get your organization going, you need a purpose that gives people a reason to hit the ground running each day. It's simple, but simple does not mean simplistic.

I used this to get kingdom results in a number of organizations over the years. Our leaders and I used this formula to increase attendance in a Sunday School program by 24 percent year over year (hitting an average of 524 weekly), turn around a network of churches (that now numbers over 140 with exponential increases in influence and income), and reverse a decline in a nonprofit organization (turning around a budget crisis and putting it on a path of continual growth). Participants in the strategy of Jesus process see it in their churches. Once you clarify your purpose, you must evaluate and align everything to it.

Try the following examples of decisions you need to make. Once you clarify your purpose, here are some questions you might need to ask:

- → Does a halfhearted youth leader help fulfill the purpose?
- → Does an underperforming administrative assistant help fulfill the purpose?
- → Does a musician who does not show up on time for practice help fulfill the purpose?
- → Does the decline in giving help fulfill the purpose?
- → Does keeping a staff member on the church's payroll to support his family fulfill the purpose?
- → Does putting up with vocally negative people because they might leave the church help to fulfill the purpose?
- → Does your unwillingness to deal with conflict help fulfill the purpose?

If any of these hypothetical scenarios are happening in your organization, you need to change them. These are heavy lifts, especially where accountability is not part of the organization's culture. I have helped many rectify problems like these, and they got results even better than they had anticipated. Using Jesus's strategy makes difficult changes much less difficult, even exciting in many instances. But they are still tough things to deal with. Often, they aren't encouraging situations. Dealing with problems saps us emotionally and creates a sense of dread.

So, here's a question: If it's uncomfortable to deal with problems, why would a leader go to the trouble of dealing with the mentioned scenarios? The answer? Your organization's purpose is most important. It's why you exist, and it makes dealing with the tough stuff worth it to the kingdom. Dealing with people within the organization is one of the hardest parts of ministry. You love them. Many are friends, close friends even. Why disrupt a relationship by requiring a leader to show up on time? Here's a principle I discovered in ministry:

*The mission is more important than the missionary.*
*The ministry is more important than the minister.*

This is a difficult principle for some to embrace. But let's put it in the context of Jesus.

Jesus suffered for His mission "to seek and to save that which was lost" (Luke 19:10, NKJV). He endured physical torture and, ultimately, death so we could experience the new birth. Jesus also confronted Peter, probably His best friend, and told him, "Get behind me, Satan" (Matthew 16:23) when Peter stood in the way of the mission.

Jesus put the mission ahead of the missionary. So should we. The question I regularly ask myself is, "Am I going to do what's easy for me, or am I going to do what is necessary to fulfill Christ's mission for this organization?"

But to make these decisions based on your purpose, you (and your leaders) must first be clear on your Organizational Purpose. Without it, you and your church leaders are left to guess how well your church is doing. But when you and your leaders collectively understand your purpose, you take the most significant step in aligning your organization to it and reduce problems as you do it. Life is too short for infighting or boring meetings.

Your Organizational Purpose includes three things:

1. Your Mission—your organization's reason for existing
2. Your Values—the guidelines that determine how you live, work, and treat each other
3. Your Vision—a clear picture of how your organization will look at some certain time in the future (three years, five years, or maybe ten years)

## Mission—The Reason Your Church/Organization Exists

Your church's mission tells you (and everybody else) why your church exists. Without this clarity, your leaders and members can still do good things. But you won't get traction or be truly effective without the "why."

Your church's mission may seem obvious to you. Chances are, if you are reading this book, you are a key leader at your church. As the key leader, you invest a lot of time thinking about the church: where are you headed, how will you get there, obstacles you must overcome, analyzing the area where your church is located to support and assist the community, and how to best use your resources (people, facilities, and money) to make the biggest impact. It may surprise you to know most people in your congregation don't think about those things.

Want to test how clear your mission is? At your next leaders' meeting, hand each participant a 3" x 5" index card. Make sure they each have a pen. Then give them this direction: "Without talking to each other, write on the index card what you believe our church's mission is. Our mission is why we exist as a church. Ready, write."

Now, if each of your key leaders writes the exact same words on each of those index cards, your mission is clear! If, however, (and I suspect this is the case unless you work on it regularly) different leaders write different statements, you know you have more work to do.

Jesus made his mission clear by involving His leaders in the discussion. I have found including your leaders on the front end of finding your mission also helps you clarify it.

A member of one of my cohorts recently asked, "Don't all churches have the same mission?" I asked him if he had any children. He did, just as most other people in the cohort indicated. "Does each one of your children have a head?" Each attendee replied in the positive. "A face?" "Yes." "A body?" Also, all yeses.

So, if all kids are basically the same, why don't we just call them all by the same name?

George Foreman tried naming all his sons (but not his daughters) the same name. If you follow professional boxing, you know Foreman to be the oldest heavyweight champion in history.[20] You might also know he has twelve children: five sons and seven daughters. He named all the sons "George." He did it "so they would always have something in common."[21] But even the boxing legend George Foreman knew those five boys were different from each other. He numbered the sons and gave each a nickname! He knew what church leaders intuitively know; churches have many similarities, but all churches are different and therefore possess a different mission. No two churches have the same people, the same pastor, or the same setting. Your church's mission should reflect these facts.

Even for our own children, we assign a different name to each one partly because the child belongs to us and because we know no two children are the same. We bear responsibility and affection for each child, so we go through the process of naming them. For the same reasons, it's important for you and your church leaders to identify and "own" your church's reason for existing. Your church is different from every other church, even though you share many things in common.

A good mission statement contains thirteen words or so. It states why your church exists. Your mission is not a paragraph; it's a simple sentence that serves as your north star to indicate where the organization is headed. Here are a couple of good ones:

→ Develop leaders to achieve kingdom results, personally and in the organizations they lead.—leaderINCREASE (a leadership development ministry)
→ To organize the world's information and make it universally accessible and useful.—Google

Even as you read these mission statements, you feel a sense of forward movement, a clear direction and path into the future.

One of the most important parts of creating a mission statement is that you do it with your key leaders. That's how Jesus did it. Jesus began the mission statement creation in Matthew 16:13 (NKJV) by taking an external opinion poll: "Who do men say that I, the Son of Man, am?" He continued by garnering input from His key leaders: "But who do you say that I am?" (Matthew 16:15, NKJV).

What was Jesus's mission? Peter said what it was, "You are the Christ, the Son of the Living God" (Matthew 16:16, NKJV). The word "Christ" in the New Testament Greek matches the word "Messiah" in Old Testament Hebrew. The word means "the Anointed One." Peter's attribution identified Jesus as the Promised One and the One God chose to save His people from their sins (Matthew 1:21). Those Jewish boys understood the gravity of the shout-out. They recognized that Jesus carried the heft of salvation when He accepted Peter's declaration. It matches Jesus's description of Himself as the One Who "came to seek and to save that which was lost" (Luke 19:10, ASV). The further recognition of Jesus as "the Son of the living God" ascribed deity to Him. In one short sentence, Peter clarified Jesus's mission. And notice this sixteenth chapter of Matthew launches the church.

Here's what Jesus did that we should do: He clarified the mission of the church with His key leaders, garnering their input.

Don't just announce it.

Don't emerge from your study and preach it.

Gather your leaders and discover it together.

# Four Advantages to Using Your Key Leaders to Clarify the Mission

## Advantage #1: Your leaders embrace the mission from day one because they participated in its discovery.

*People Own What They Create.*

What if I hand you a book on leadership and tell you it's a wonderful book and that if you simply do what's in the book, it will revolutionize your leadership skills? You may have questions about it, but it might sit on your nightstand with your other piles of "need to read" books.

However, what if you and I wrote a book on leadership, taking all we learned and gleaning insight from other great leaders? You would believe it's a great book on leadership. You would probably tell others, give it away to struggling pastors, and most likely teach what's in the book.

Crazy thought here, what if the book you wrote contained the same information as the book I tried to give you?

What would be the difference? *You created the one you believe in.*

It's the same with your people. Let them participate in the creation, and they will own it. If you construct a statement and then try to get them to embrace it, you'll spend a lot of time answering questions that you avoid when they help on the front end.

Here are samples of questions (and time) you avoid by involving your leaders in the discovery process:

→ "Does this mean we aren't going to do X anymore?"

→ "How about so-and-so's group. Will that change?"

→ "When did we decide that?"

→ "Are we doing this now?"

→ "What about . . .?"

→ "How will this affect . . .?"

→ "Does that mean . . .?"

And on it goes.

You avoid a lot of confusion by involving your leaders. You also get questions and insights you didn't think of (ask me how I know).

## Advantage #2: You begin with a coalition of ambassadors.

When you involve your key leaders in the mission creation process, you jumpstart the communication. Those leaders share the same language and have the same heart because they worked together to discover the mission. Conversely, if the leader alone comes up with a mission (or a vision), you then must tell somebody. That somebody will have questions, seek insight, and need some sort of background to understand it. When you create the mission by yourself, you'll spend a lot of time explaining, re-explaining, clarifying, and attempting to get people on board with the mission. But if you use Jesus's method by including a group of ten to twelve leaders in the process, you multiply your efforts by a factor of ten to twelve right out of the gate.

And what's more, those ten to twelve own it and understand it. When you start with your leaders as part of the process, you don't just begin with spokespeople. Your starters, who have great backgrounds and can answer questions, are now ambassadors for what God wants to do.

## Advantage #3: You begin with momentum.

Having facilitated this process umpteen times, I can feel the sense of momentum it creates just by typing this. Energy, excitement, and a "Wow, here we go!" accompany this initial push. As the key leader of an area within the church twice (as a youth leader in a church of about 350 in attendance and as a maturity/ministry leader in a church of around 5,000 in attendance), a leader of a network of churches, a nonprofit, and then several times helping other organizations (church, nonprofit, for-profit), this momentum happens every . . . single . . . time. It's also a lot of fun.

## Advantage #4: It takes less time to implement.

It doesn't take long. You can craft your mission statement in an initial four-hour session, a two-hour writing sub-team meeting, and a thirty-minute check-in with the lead team. That's it. As an alternative, if you create the statement within the strategy of Jesus process (which takes two days), we get the statement on the first day.

Compare this to a leader who told me, "After two years, we finally have our mission clearly written." Which would you choose? If He had taken two years to write His mission for the church, He would only have had one year to work it. Time is of the essence, even if you aren't Jesus. Psalm 90:12 (NASB) instructs us, "So teach us to number our days, That we may present to You a heart of wisdom."

What's striking is how different Jesus's approach was from how most churches operate. Many church leaders believe you should just "tell" them why your church exists. They also (falsely) think the people in their church will then magically do three things after you tell them:

1. Understand what you are saying
2. Believe what you are saying
3. Implement what you are saying

Jesus did not make these assumptions. He did not leave communicating His mission to only Him saying it. Because He wanted them to understand, internalize, and implement His mission, He led them to discover the answer themselves. Like Jesus, your mission is clear when you involve your leaders in discovering it.

***In addition to your church's mission, great leaders clarify the values of the organization.***

## Values: Fundamental Traits of How We Operate

A six-foot, eight-inch-tall gentleman confronted me in the church hallway just after a leaders' meeting where we had announced yet another change.

He looked down at me and said, "Is this (new schedule, new rooms) how it's going to be from now on?"

"How long have you been going to church here?" I asked.

"Seventeen years," he said.

"Have things ever stayed the same for very long?"

"You're right," he said and walked away satisfied.

In that church, we used to hear a lot from people (unprompted), "(Our church), where change is your friend." The big guy's satisfaction after our brief interaction in the hallway showed he inherently knew "continual change" was one of our values. Our values show up throughout our organizations. Your values show your marching orders in your day-to-day life. Every person and all organizations have them, written or not. If you don't write your values, they aren't clear, and you increase the likelihood people will violate them. When your values are unclear, your church will struggle with her culture.

To help this, many churches nowadays require a membership class before someone joins the church. The main value in these membership classes is to get agreement about the church's values (which also reflect doctrine) before the person becomes a member. When done well, these classes clarify the expectations of church membership on the front end.

For example, when our church taught these classes, one of the things we included was the fact that our church always wanted to grow. "The church exists for those who are not yet part of it," was one of our tenets. We wanted people to know the church exists for those who are lost, without Christ. The church does not exist for those who are already part of the church. Of course, we also discipled people and worshiped, but our key focus was those outside the body of Christ.

Can you see how important this is? If somebody joins our church thinking it's for the members, they likely will be upset when we change the schedule, move rooms around, raise money, and change the church's location to reach more people. If you make it clear on the front end that we will do whatever we need to do to reach people, then people may still be a bit frustrated, but we clarified the expectations on the front end.

Writing and clarifying your values define your culture and keep it consistent. Although there is no magic number, landing on five to eight key values usually works best for most organizations.

## How to Use Your Values

You use them when making staffing decisions. They guide you in handling conflict. If one of your values is "dignity of the individual," for example, you won't tolerate a staff person who treats members or other staff with disrespect. You won't hire people who make snarky comments about other people, what those people are wearing, where they are from, their income level, etc. A value is an inviolable border you won't transgress.

# Vision: Seeing Where We Will Be

A vision is only a vision when others can see it.

Jesus shared His in Matthew: "For the Son of Man is going to come in his Father's glory with his angels, and then he will reward each person according to what they have done. Truly, I tell you, some who are standing here will not taste death before they see the Son of Man coming in his kingdom" (Matthew 16:27–28). Jesus painted a picture of a preferred future. His vision showed His disciples what would happen as they fulfilled the mission. So should ours.

While your mission forms the reason for your existence, your vision shows what that mission looks like at a certain point in the future if it goes well. Typically, I use ten years. Then you develop your three- and five-year mile markers. Your mile markers show where you need to be at the three- and five-year marks to achieve your ten-year vision. Anything beyond ten years will likely change too much to be useful.

Effective leaders base vision in their mission, their reason for existing. A vision takes the mission into the future and describes how their church will look, feel, and sound at a future-appointed time. You know you possess a clear vision when people can "see" what you describe. If you use a "vision statement," here's the question your statement must answer: Can people see it?

For example, Stowe Mission of Central Ohio functions as one of the leading nonprofits in Columbus, Ohio, our nation's fourteenth largest city. Stowe Mission serves under-resourced people. Stowe currently provides a free dental clinic, vision clinic, food pantry, community kitchen, pregnancy resource center, mental health program, after-school program, block parties, spiritual direction, and emotional support. We also facilitate several other services. When I became CEO, my first organizational step was to clarify the mission. Using the process described in this book, we determined that "Stowe Mission exists to give gospel hope and restoration to people facing hardships."

It looks simple but a lot is packed into it. We are "gospel-focused" (which was one of our criteria for the statement). Notice also that we help people "facing" hardship. They are "up against it." These are not "hardship people" or "people with hardships." This nuance follows our core value of the "dignity of people."

So, that's the mission. But what is the vision? In Stowe's situation, our vision only required a few words added to the mission. If you have seen Stowe Mission and our campus, you "see" what we do. Here's what we did for the vision:

Give gospel hope and restoration to people facing hardship *in multiple locations and satellites.*

The vision is to do what we are doing in our current 15,000-square-foot facility in additional places. A location will be another facility about the same size that also fulfills the mission. A satellite, on the other hand, is where we resource an existing ministry with the processes and resources we have.

| Location | Satellite |
|---|---|
| We own the building. | We do not own the building. |
| We provide the staff. | We do not provide on-site staff, although our staff help. |
| We pay the utilities and insurance. | The sponsoring ministry/church pays for the utilities and insurance. |
| We initiate spiritual engagements with the people who come. | The staff at the sponsoring ministry/church initiates spiritual engagements. |
| For the people who want to know more, we direct them to the church that meets on our campus. | We encourage our satellites to direct people to their church. |

You can "see" this, which makes it a vision. To show how potent a clear vision is, fifteen months after launching a clear vision, a church voted unanimously to donate their entire $1.5 million property to our ministry. It's the largest single gift we have received to date. That could not have happened without a clear, compelling vision based solidly on our mission.

It happened over lunch with a lay leader on May 17. As he shared his church's situation, I referred him to the vision. He remembered seeing the document and the video. His church voted unanimously on October 24 of that same year to give the property to us. It's the power of vision. And what's better, anybody can do it. Yes, pastor, you can do it. Furthermore, pastor, God wants you to pursue a vision.

Clarify your church's purpose (with your leaders), work it, craft a crystal-clear compelling vision, and watch God supply the resources to achieve it.

*The resources only show up when the vision is clear.*

In summary, a strategic leader begins by establishing these three keys: Mission, Values, and Vision. You can use this foundation to build a great church, company, or ministry. This starts the process, but there's more to come.

Next, you need a plan.

*Chapter 13*

# ORGANIZATIONAL PLAN

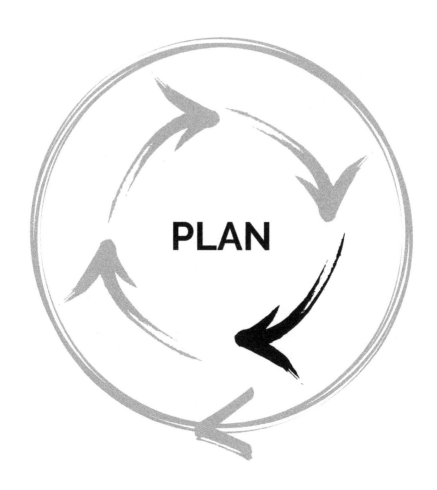

 <!-- contains the word PLAN inside circular arrows -->

PLAN

*"The great thing is to be found at one's post as a child of God,
living each day as though it were our last, but planning as though
our world might last a hundred years."*
—C.S. Lewis, *God in the Dock*

# Every Purpose Needs a Plan to Achieve It

*"Without good advice everything goes wrong—
it takes careful planning for things to go right."*
—Proverbs 15:22 (CEV)

Time away was long overdue. Too much work and not enough downtime spurred me to book three days to Costa Rica for my wife, Tina, and me. We got the flights, booked a hotel, and reserved a car. Sounds like a plan, doesn't it? Not quite.

It didn't hit me until we got our rental car that I didn't know how to get to our hotel. My phone didn't work out of the country. The Spanish speaker at the rental counter gave me the keys to the rental car. With my limited Spanish, I explained our problem. So he pulled out a paper map and wrote a big "H" where the hotel was. Then he circled where we were. Here we go!

Until we discovered the map was totally in Spanish.

The Spanish word for "hotel" is "hotel," by the way. So the momentary comfort of seeing him put an "H" where the hotel was quickly evaporated. We eventually made it to the hotel after driving two hours in the wrong direction, which added four hours to the trip. But even with going the wrong way, the right map helped us get to our destination safely.

Too many churches operate the way I "planned" the trip. First, they create a big idea and handle a few big-picture items. Then they wonder why they get lackluster results. Without a plan, a grand vision only brings disappointment.

Big ideas only bring big results when translated into a plan that facilitates them. If left in the vision stage, few people know where they can contribute, even when they want to help.

Jesus had a plan. After his key leaders clarified His purpose in Matthew, He said: "From then on Jesus began to point out to his disciples that it was necessary for him to go to Jerusalem and suffer many things from the elders, chief priests, and scribes, be killed, and be raised the third day" (Matthew 16:21, CSB).

*Because Jesus enacted a plan, so should we.*

> *"Make no little plans; they have no magic to stir men's blood, and probably themselves will not be realized. Make big plans; aim high in hope and work, remembering that a noble, logical diagram once recorded will never die, but long after, we are gone be a living thing, asserting itself with ever-growing insistency. Remember that our sons and our grandsons are going to do things that would stagger us. Let your watchword be order and your beacon beauty."*
> —Daniel Burnham, *Plan of Chicago*

# What Is a Ministry Action Plan (MAP)?

To build an effective ministry, clarify your purpose (mission, vision, and values), build a Ministry Action Plan, and follow it. You do this by gathering your leaders to determine the best way to achieve the purpose God gave you and your church.

Like my time in Costa Rica, you need a MAP (Ministry Action Plan) to achieve your purpose. Your MAP is the roadmap to follow to reach the destination of your mission/vision. Without it, you and your leaders will waste a lot of time meandering through meetings and decisions and "hope-so" thinking. With it, you make clear, definitive steps to achieve God's best. A good MAP creates a sense of momentum and positive anticipation about the future.

When we see a map of a city, we know somebody drew it. For your church's (or organization's) map, you are the "map drawer." You create the MAP using seven elements to DRAW (the) MAP. All seven are necessary to get where your purpose says you want to be. The seven elements are a **D**eadline, **R**eviewed, **A**ccountable, **W**ritten, **M**easurable, **A**ctionable, and **P**urpose.

**D**eadline

**R**eviewed

**A**ctionable

**W**ritten

**M**easurable

**A**ccountable

**P**urposeful

You become the cartographer for the journey to fulfilling Christ's purpose for your church. A "plan" without these specific seven elements lacks enough clarity to be a strong MAP. Leave out any one element and the results suffer.

## How to DRAW (the) MAP

You can use a MAP for planning at any level in your church, but first, owning a clear purpose (mission, vision, values) will give you the best results. To be effective, a MAP includes:

## Deadline

How many times have you said, "Let's get together some time?" And your friend says, "Absolutely. We need to do that." Then months and years pass with no connection. Why? You didn't set a date. What does not get calendared does not get done. It's true of lunch with friends. It's also true with ideas churches have. A lot of time and energy can be saved by asking, "When will we do that?"

A deadline commits you to action. Without a deadline, ideas drag and eventually die. For a MAP, you need the date the particular action step will be completed. Done. Finished. If you need to bring back a report or make further decisions, include those items in the process of creating a deadline. But it's best to not make research or further discussion the deadline. Basing your deadline on a report prolongs the timeline and puts off what you really want, which is a result.

One group told me they wanted their deadline to be TBD (To Be Determined). I said, "Okay, so let's determine it now. What date will we pick?" And they chose a deadline. Sometimes you need to do a little nudging to get specific. But the results are worth it.

## Reviewed

What do you call a plan that is only in the head of the pastor? *A secret.*

People cannot execute what they cannot see. Having some ideas and sharing them at a meeting usually does not give tangible results. Brainstorming can be a good starter, but you need the insight and input of others to make it effective for the ministry. When your key leaders see it, then they can implement it. If you create the MAP by yourself, you disallow the available momentum and execution that comes by including your team. When a plan is "reviewed," all your leaders see it. It's even stronger when your leaders not only see it but participate in the plan's creation. When they see it, they not only understand their roles, they see how their functions interact with the others.

***You can meet without leading, but you cannot lead without meeting.***

Planning requires focused time with your key leaders to develop a written plan for action.

## Accountable

*If more than one person is accountable, nobody is accountable.*

Being accountable means one person is in charge of accomplishing a certain action. Avoid confusion and finger-pointing by determining one leader. Then give that leader the authority to lead the endeavor. After all, you cannot be accountable for what you cannot control. Never start a ministry without a minister. If you do begin a ministry without a clearly defined leader, the pastor winds up taking responsibility for it. Effective leaders empower others and don't continually take on new projects themselves. It may be a lay leader or a ministerial staff person, but you need one (and only one) person leading any ministry, event, or action step.

## Written

*A good clear plan is written.*

Why write it?

Habakkuk 2:2–4 (NKJV) says: "Then the Lord answered me and said: 'Write the vision and make it plain on tablets, that he may run who reads it. For the vision is yet for an appointed time; but at the end it will speak, and it will not lie. Though it tarries, wait for it; because it will surely come, it will not tarry. Behold the proud, His soul is not upright in him; but the just shall live by his faith.'"

**Writing makes it clear.** ("make it plain" verse 2)

As Dawson Trotman said, "Thoughts disentangle themselves when they pass through the lips and the fingertips." If it isn't written, it isn't as clear as it could be. When you write it, it becomes clearer to you and to others.

**The people in your organization can run when they see ("read") it.** Writing shows a level of commitment deeper than the spoken word. Words we speak can be forgotten, misinterpreted, or discounted because nobody remembers 100 percent of what was said.

On the other hand,

→ Writing is more formal. People tend to take more seriously what is written.

→ Writing is more deliberate. It requires clarifying your thinking to be accurate.

→ Writing takes more time. Slowing the process, even if only a skosh, forces deeper mental processing.

→ Writing has a higher level of commitment. People won't remember exactly what you said. They can forever see what you write.

→ Writing does not fade like the memory of what you or someone else said.

→ Writing is clearer.

***You are more likely to achieve goals that are written.***

Writing a goal makes you 42 percent more likely to achieve it, according to Dr. Gail Matthews, a psychology professor at Dominican University in California.[22] That alone makes it worth inking.

## Measurable

How do we know there were 3,000 people at Pentecost? Somebody counted the people. Why did they count? I think they counted because they cared about those souls.

Proverbs tells us to "know the state of your flocks, and put your heart into caring for your herds" (Proverbs 27:23, NLT). The New Testament echoes this sentiment in Acts: "Pay careful attention to yourselves and to all the flock, in which the Holy Spirit has made you overseers, to care for the church of God, which he obtained with his own blood" (Acts 20:28, ESV). It seems difficult, if not impossible, to care for the flock if I don't know how many sheep I have.

Notice also how Jesus measured in Matthew 16:27 (CSB), "then he will reward each according to what he has done." As churches, we tend to shy away from measuring performance. But Jesus measured results. He not only measured behavior, but He also rewarded behavior: "he will reward each according to what he has done." Then again, in the Parable of the Talents in Matthew 25, the master based his response on what the servant accomplished. This passage is the one I hear most quoted when encouraging people to be faithful to the end of their lives.

We all want to hear, "Well done, good and faithful servant" (Matthew 25:21). But Jesus only said that to the servants who produced measurable results. The master knew the servants produced because he counted the number of talents they achieved. To the servant who did not produce, the master said, "You wicked and lazy servant" (Matthew 25:26, NKJV). It may seem harsh to us, but it was important to Jesus, as He showed in the parable.

The Measurable element in DRAWMAP includes knowing how much money it will take to do any project. Luke 14:28 (NLT) tells us, "But don't begin until you count the cost. For who would begin construction of a building without first calculating the cost to see if there is enough money to finish it?"

Do you measure performance? How well are your small group leaders leading? What empirical evidence do you regularly collect to tell you how well they are doing? You may think, "Well, people seem to be enjoying it." While that may be true, people's enjoyment doesn't (by itself) determine if the person is doing a good job. Jesus measured and evaluated people's behavior. If we are strategic in accomplishing what He gave us to do, we will also measure performance.

## Actionable

Start each action with an action verb. Avoid verbs like "Study" or "Research" or "Look into." Instead, focus on action. Do. Take the hill. Stretch what you think is possible and go for it. You will learn things by going for it that no amount of noodling could create.

## Purpose–Connected

Our network of churches determined our mission to be to "resource, connect, plant, and encourage pastors and churches."

I got a call a few years after we decided our mission from the campaign co-chair of a gubernatorial candidate. The candidate and I attended a couple of lunches together. He spoke well, and his values aligned with mine. I voted for the guy. The co-chair asked if I could "get some pastors together to meet him." Since it involved our churches, it needed to fit our mission for me to participate. So I used our mission to guide my thinking.

Would this meeting resource churches? No.

Could it connect churches? No.

Might it plant or encourage pastors or churches? No.

So I didn't do it. I did not participate because it did not solidly fit what we said we do. Here's a less than funny joke for you: What do you call an action not attached to your purpose? *Not helpful.*

It's not helpful and is typically a distraction because you could have used the time, effort, and energy of your people to accomplish something that does move toward your purpose. The event itself may be very good, as was the meeting with the potential governor. But if the event/meeting does not fulfill your organization's reason for existing, don't do it.

So, to create a good MAP, you need to **DRAWMAP**.

Here's a fuller layout that I started using in the late 1990s with my staff. I would write it on a large piece of paper and leave it hanging in our weekly meeting space. It served as a continual reminder of what we are doing, who is responsible, and when it is due.

| MINISTRY ACTION PLAN (M.A.P.) | | | | LEADER INCREASE |
|---|---|---|---|---|
| **WHO**<br>One Person<br>Responsible | **WHY**<br>Objective (connected<br>to Purpose) | **WHAT**<br>Expected Outcomes | **WHEN**<br>Due Date | **HOW MUCH**<br>Cost |
| | | | | |

It gets you from here to there.

When you plan, you DRAW(the)MAP to get where you want to go. Your mission/vision identifies the destination. Then your MAP shows the routes you and your team take to arrive there.

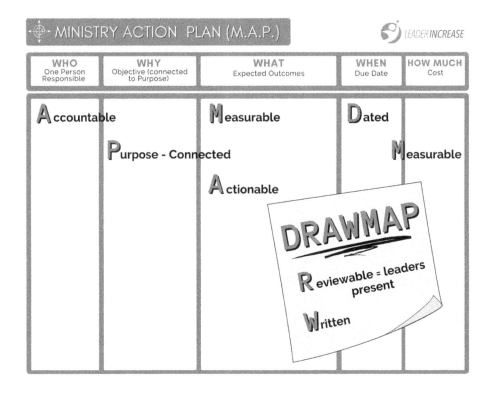

## What Happens Without a Plan?

> *"The plans of the diligent lead surely to abundance, but everyone who is hasty comes only to poverty."*
> —Proverbs 21:5 (ESV)

→ Time gets wasted in meetings pinging back and forth between the 30,000-foot view of "we need more people" and the boots-on-the-ground perspective of "who's bringing the nachos for the Fall Festival?"

→ The ministry lacks direction. People don't know where the whole thing is headed. A few might see it. But churches limit their potential by not identifying the desired destination. Would you get on a plane if you didn't know where it was headed?

→ Great leaders in your church hesitate to participate because they don't want to be frustrated by not having a plan.

→ The church struggles to get volunteers. A "volunteer problem" can be due to a lack of planning. People don't help because they don't know where or how to help. If you find yourself saying, "I need some help!" instead of a specific, plan-fulfilling request like "I need a youth committee member who handles the finances," for example, you may need to give more attention to planning.

→ The ministry has "communication problems." Most churches I help list this as one of their most persistent problems. "Nobody told me this room was scheduled for the Burke's fiftieth anniversary party" is an example of what poses as a communication problem. But in reality, churches don't have communication problems; they have planning problems. In the example of the anniversary party, if the church followed a good strategic rhythm where the leaders met monthly to evaluate progress and look at the upcoming calendar, they would have seen the room conflict long before it occurred. Somewhere along the way, they would have developed a scheduling system (analog or digital) so all the leaders could know who was meeting where. It really wasn't a communication problem. It was a planning problem.

→ You feel frustrated (and maybe discouraged) because you feel like it all falls on your shoulders.

---

**Communication problems mask organizational confusion that good planning resolves.**

---

→ Problems increase. You maintain and increase momentum when you plan and things go well. Momentum solves a lot of problems. The church where I served as youth pastor didn't love the cake icing on the floor when we decorated kids' faces like cakes at a youth event. But because we gained so many teenagers, it really wasn't a big deal. (I also apologized profusely to the janitor. For the next events, we made sure we cleaned everything before finishing.) But without momentum, seemingly small issues get big.

→ The ministry does not consistently improve. You may see some good things happen. A few people get saved one week. Somebody wanted to feed the homeless, so we did it, and that was good. A new family showed up. A long-time member died, so the church supplied the meal after the funeral, and we felt good that we could help. These are all good things, but we miss the steadily improving effectiveness an overall plan brings.

Life and ministry do not have to be this way. Good planning prevents a lot of pain.

## What Happens with a Plan?

→ The ministry steadily improves. As you clarify your purpose, evaluate and retool your plan, do the work, format the organization, and establish an improvement rhythm, your ministry gets better. This process systematically ratchets up your entire organization.

→ You save time in meetings. Once you establish the big picture issues (mission, vision, and values) for the year and spend your monthly meetings executing that plan, you save time. For example, when someone asks a big picture question in your monthly meetings like, "We need to do more evangelism." You say, "We covered how we will do evangelism this year in our annual planning meeting. Right now, we are working to make this next evangelism project the best we can. Once it's over, we will evaluate it (and the other evangelism projects) at our next annual planning meeting to see if we want to keep these, retool them, or try something different." Without a plan, you and your team will hear a statement like, "We need to do more evangelism," and waste time talking about it when you should be planning the next event. If you have ten people in a room and waste thirty minutes talking about off-task issues, you just wasted five whole hours. And not only did you waste five hours, but you also lost five hours of people's time, which did not help you plan the next event.

→ You possess ease in leading. With good planning, you live with day-to-day comfort, knowing where your ministry is going and how to get there. Ministry has enough of its own challenges without adding to it by not having a good plan. Good planning increases the church's effectiveness and decreases your personal frustration.

→ Your leadership influence grows. The longer you stay at a place, the more credibility you should have. The longer you remain in a ministry, the bigger the objectives you can achieve. But this only happens with a plan. Without a plan, you'll wonder why things aren't going well.

→ You see God do what only God can do. And this is the point, isn't it? This is the ultimate aim. It may seem counterintuitive, but the people who see God do what only God can do are planners. They discern His direction and then embark on a plan to fulfill it. I have seen it in the lives of other leaders and even in my own life. I would not want to live any other way.

*"Small plans at best yield small results, and big plans at worst beat small plans. So, when I want big results, I need a big plan. The best outcomes—in any of life's endeavors—are almost always the result of a big plan powered by persistent effort over time. That approach will not only give you the best possible chance to win, it will also put you in the best possible position to win big."*
—Gary Keller, *The Millionaire Real Estate Investor*

After you DRAWMAP, know you still have further to go. Once the plan gets installed, it's time to do the work.

## Chapter 14

# ORGANIZATIONAL WORK

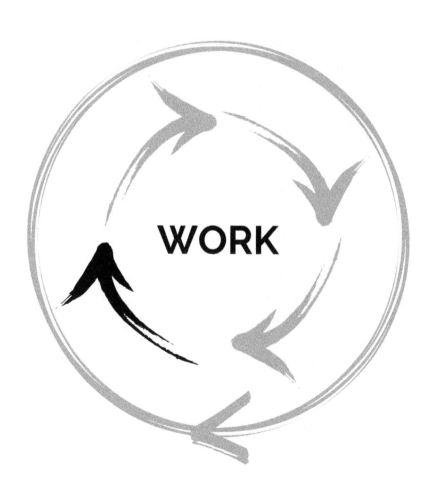

*"People often ask me if I know the secret of success and if I could tell others how to make their dreams come true. My answer is, you do it by working."*
—Walt Disney


*"At least move around. You're killing the grass."*
—Football Coach at South Point High School


## Spanish Flash Cards

Spanish seemed like an important class. In my sophomore year of college, nine of us went to Coatzacoalcos, Mexico, to work with an international mission agency. Once we got there, my team included people from Brazil, Mexico, Malaysia, Sweden, and the United States. As we visited one of the churches, our group prayed in Mandarin, Spanish, Portuguese, Swedish, and English. Wow! God immediately got bigger in my mind. Hearing people talking to God in so many languages escalated my view of the vastness of God. The God of all these languages sees through a lens much larger and more multi-faceted than I imagined.

So when I returned to Berea College, I wanted to learn more. One of my dormmates participated in the same Spanish class I took. As I entered the lobby one day, he worked his way through his note cards to learn the language, Spanish on one side and English on the other. The problem was the English word on the front of the card did not match the Spanish word on the back of the card. The same was true of the next card and the next. Very few English words on the front of the cards matched the Spanish words on the backs of those cards. He worked, but that particular work did not help him learn Spanish.

**Doing the wrong thing can hurt more than help,
even when the intentions are good.**

*"One who is slack in his work is brother to one who destroys."*
—Proverbs 18:9

## What Is Work?

*"You can't build a reputation on what you're going to do."*
—Henry Ford

To effectively execute a plan, you must do two things:

1. Work
2. Do the work that advances the mission

Churches typically engage in a lot of activity. But the work that really helps them is only work directed toward fulfilling the mission. Misdirected action won't produce the desired results. So, when someone in your church says, "I feel led to . . ." it's important to determine whether or not that action moves toward your mission. If what they want to do advances the mission, you should do it.

Conversely, if what one member wants to do does not advance the mission, your church would best avoid it. I once had a church member schedule a meeting with me because he felt led to start a Christian Bar Mitzvah. We met for breakfast. I shared a few written questions for him to complete indicating whether or not what he felt led to do matched our mission. He never answered the questions. Honestly, I'm still not sure what he had in mind. But I know our church saved a lot of time, effort, and focus by not pursuing it.

*"I must work the works of Him who sent Me."*
—John 9:4 (NKJV)

When Jesus said, "I must work," He tells us even He had to work to see God's kingdom advanced. But notice He further qualified what work He did. He said He must work "the works of Him who sent Me." This shows us Jesus only did certain kinds of work. And the work the Son of God did advance His mission, the mission of the church. Jesus's works were the "works of Him who sent Me." Not all works are.

---

### Misdirected actions won't produce the desired results.

---

There's a time to plan and a time to work. Although planning feels like work, it is not the work. Planning is preparation for work. Planning and strategizing are necessary, but by themselves don't get the job done. Another way of saying it is the meeting is not the ministry. The meeting can prepare for ministry, but in and of itself, meetings don't produce ministry results. Be wary of too much planning. You want to plan enough to get going and to deal with obstacles. But don't invest too much time trying to answer all the questions. Many questions won't get discovered, let alone answered, until you're doing the work.

Too many huddles mean you never run the play. Equally as damaging is the other extreme of "just do it." Your doing only helps when your actions strongly support the mission.

A pastor told me, "I didn't know what to do, so I just started knocking on doors." In his context, it did not produce ministry results because nobody ever answered the door when he knocked on them. As my seminary personal evangelism professor said, "God is not honored by wasting gasoline."

*God gives the birds their food, but He doesn't throw it into their nests.*

Let's take a glance at a group of people God used in amazing, effective ways. Some call it the "Roll Call of Faith" in Hebrews 11.

By faith Abel offered . . . (v. 4)

By faith Enoch pleased God . . . (v. 5)

By faith Noah built . . . (v. 7)

By faith Abraham obeyed and went . . . (v. 8)

By faith Abraham offered . . . (v. 17)

By faith Isaac blessed . . . (v. 20)

By faith Jacob blessed and worshiped (v. 21)

By faith Joseph spoke . . . (v. 22)

By faith Moses' parents hid . . . (v. 23)

By faith Moses refused . . . (v. 24)

By faith he (Moses) left . . . (v. 27)

By faith the people passed . . . (v. 29)

By faith the walls of Jericho fell after the people had marched . . . (v. 30)

By faith the prostitute Rahab welcomed . . . (v. 31)

Notice two things:

1.  Each person God used worked. They acted. They did something.
2.  The people God used acted according to what God wanted to accomplish. They took certain actions, not just any actions. They acted in a way that aligned with faith. Not all actions do.

Recognizing that we must work to be effective, what kinds of work should we do? Do the work that supports your purpose (your mission, vision, and values).

> *"For we are His workmanship, created in Christ Jesus for good works,*
> *which God prepared beforehand that we should walk in them."*
> —Ephesians 2:10 (NKJV)

# Chapter 15

# ORGANIZATIONAL FORMAT –YOUR SYSTEM AND PROCESSES

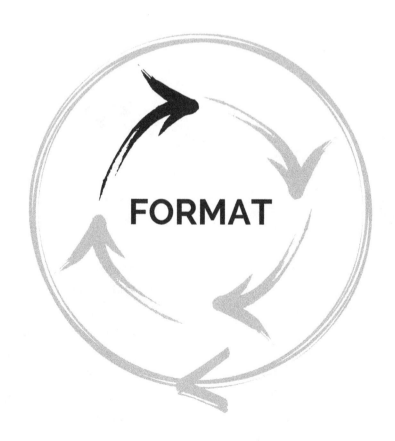

*"You either control people's behavior, or you control the format.*
*And you cannot control people's behavior."*
—Morris Owen

## Walk Around the Furniture

I f you entered the room below, where would you walk? Around the furniture. Why? Because you naturally follow a format someone else created. You don't argue about it, and you don't rearrange the furniture. You follow what is already in place.

Take a step back for a minute. Think about what the room was like before any furniture populated it. It's pretty much a blank slate. Without furniture, we see the room itself. The windows, the walkway into the living room, and the stairwell are (relatively) fixed. So we know we need to place the sofa, loveseat, chairs, and coffee and sofa tables to accommodate what is there. But you can pick whatever furniture you want. And you can arrange the furniture you pick however you decide.

Based on your decisions and what you put in place, people entering that room walk around the furniture you chose. When you pick the furniture and its placement, you also choose the behavior format for the people who will occupy the space. They sit where you want them to sit because of where you put the chairs, loveseat, and sofas. They walk where you decided they would walk because you created the walkway into and through the room. If you did an even more extensive format change, you could move the stairwell, the entry, and the windows. Nothing in this room is permanently fixed. When you choose the format, you choose people's behavior. People naturally adapt to the format.

God used this same format principle with Abram, and Jesus used it with Peter. Your leadership will improve if you use it, too.

## People Follow Formats

---

Your format is how your organization, teams, systems, and processes are structured.

---

Let's look at how God (in the Old Testament) created a format that a believer behaved in. When God encountered Abram, He did not ask for a mindset change. Instead, He gave Abram a promise, but the promise was preceded by a family move out of his country:

> "The Lord had said to Abram, 'Leave your native country, your relatives, and your father's family, and go to the land that I will show you. I will make you into a great nation. I will bless you and make you famous, and you will be a blessing to others. I will bless those who bless you and curse those who treat you with contempt. All the families on earth will be blessed through you.' So Abram departed as the Lord had instructed, and Lot went with him. Abram was seventy-five years old when he left Haran."
> —Genesis 12:1–5 (NLT)

---

Abram's growth to Abraham required a new spatial format.

---

Notice how God changed Abram's future. He did not just give him new information or a book on leadership. To embrace God's promise, Abram had to physically leave the country where he grew up. God required Abram to move away, *even though he did not know where he was going.* This flies in the face of a church's "We need to figure it all out before we do anything" mentality. God changed Abram's life and his destiny, and even his name, but it required Abram to move out of the country.

Notice three things about Abram's new format:

1.  God put Abram in a different place to do a different thing.
2.  Abram had to reformat some relationships for God to do greater things.
3.  After the moves, God changed his name to match the new thing.

---

**Peter's growth from unpredictable to pillar required a new mental format.**

---

A second example from the New Testament shows us how Jesus created a new format to transform a follower. If you have heard or preached many sermons about the Apostle Peter, those homilies likely included words like "waffler," "undependable," or "put his foot in his mouth." Pastors typically portray Peter as fickle. Yet just a short time after the gospels, Galatians 2:9 says the early church thought of him as a "pillar." What changed him?

When Jesus first met Simon, He created a new format for him. John 1:42 tells us, "Jesus looked at him and said, 'You are Simon, son of John. You will be called Cephas' (which, when translated, is Peter). Jesus said, "Your name is Rock," when Simon (Peter) was anything but a rock. But Jesus positioned Peter to behave like a rock because Jesus and others kept calling him a rock. Jesus also mentored him and corrected him. But don't underestimate the impact of Jesus looking at you and saying, "Rock." Jesus gave Simon a new name to prompt new behavior.

What do you want the people in your organization to be?

Here's one I heard yesterday: "I told them last Sunday in the message they need to Preach the Word." I told the pastor I didn't know what he meant. When I asked him, he explained he wanted the people in his church to ask how they could pray for various individuals in their lives. Okay. I get that. But he didn't tell them that. The church did not set up any framework for comprehending what the preacher meant. When we just "tell" people, we expect them to understand what we are saying, somehow determine what it means, and then act. "Preach the Word" sounds like they should set up a pulpit in their living room or on the street corner. Whereas when you create a new format, not only do they understand what you want, you give them a clear, practical framework to follow. Compare "Preach the Word" to getting people to do what that young pastor actually wanted, which was to have them tell others about Jesus. Here's one potential format with a progression of clear actions you could use to lead others to "Preach the Word:"

→ Gather ten of your key leaders around a table and tell them "Preach the Word" means sharing the gospel with others and inviting them to church. Choose one of them (and only one) as the key leader.

→ Gather ideas with those ten key leaders about how to best help people share the gospel and invite people to church. Cull the list to the five best ideas.

→ Preach a sermon on "Preach the Word" and include the five ideas in the sermon notes.

→ In the message, tell them the kind of behavior you want in practical, observable terms. Refer to the five ideas in the sermon notes.

→ During the message, model a typical interaction you want people to have. Role-play connecting with someone and asking how to pray for them.

→ Ask for those who want to "Preach the Word" to sign a card (which you previously prepared that says what "Preach the Word" means) saying they will do it. Do this during the message. Hand in the cards at the end of the message.

→ Your key leader that you chose at the first step follows up midweek with the people who committed (via the card) to encourage and remind them. They might email or call. If you have a lot of responses, enlist a team to do the follow-up with you.

→ Next week, ask the people who "Preached the Word" to stand during the message and celebrate their actions by clapping for them.

→ Additionally, in your small groups, have each leader share how she or he "Preached the Word" using the five ideas.

For this young pastor, "Preach the Word" seemed to be an important ongoing piece of what he wanted the church to do. If that is the case, you format it. So, beyond the steps above, you assign the "Preach the Word" to a staff member or key lay leader. It could be the one who led this process if it went exceptionally well. If this process did not go well under the leader that you first chose, you might choose a different leader. You give that leader clear, measurable, defined outcomes. For example, "We want an increasing number of people who 'Preach the Word' every week." Then the leader must develop a system for ensuring it happens.

The five ideas you and your team choose to show people how to "Preach the Word" will create a more positive impact than just telling them to "Preach the Word" and hope they figure it out and do it. Creating a format for "Preach the Word" by gathering your leaders, appointing one key leader, determining the desired outcomes, and then following up and measuring results will give you a much greater impact than just mentioning it in a sermon.

Here are some global ideas about how to think "format" instead of getting people to change their behavior.

1. Don't reorder steps in an existing process. Reformat the means to achieve the desired end state.
2. Don't replace staff (paid or volunteer) with the same responsibilities as the staff who left. Reformat the position to give you more of what you want.
3. Don't rename the organization (church). Rework what you do. Once it is newly installed, you can rename it.
4. Don't rewrite the rules (or constitution). Reformat the work. Once the bugs are worked out, rewrite the rules (or constitution) to match the proven format.
5. Don't vote on committees. Don't create new committees. Enlist a leader and a team to do the work.
6. Don't think "formula," think "format," which will be a step toward your preferred future.
7. Don't think "formal," think "format." You don't have to officially change someone's title and job description to get something done. Often, it's

better if you first enlist them in the task. When you see someone actually doing the job, you can better assess if you need to formalize it (by changing their title and job description).

Installing a new format makes the change "real" and workable. You move the idea from theory and discussions to a framework for accomplishment.

## How You Know What Format You Need

Before deciding on the format, you (and your leaders) need to know where you are headed. Without a clear destination, you cannot know what format to choose. Knowing where you are headed requires a desirable "future state." The preferred future is a clear, high-definition picture of where the church will be when she accomplishes her mission at a certain point in the future. The preferred future is the vision, which is part of your purpose. It all ties together.

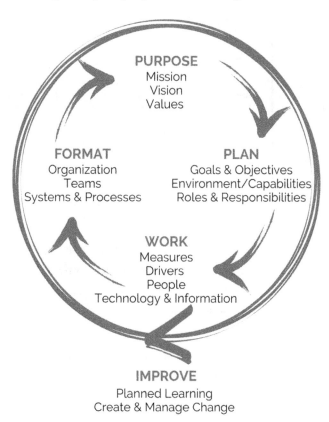

# Format of the Top Twelve (Apostles)

A soft perusal of the gospels looks like Jesus used twelve key people to advance the kingdom. A closer look shows He utilized a format inside the twelve to make His work more effective. We should do the same.

Let's take a look at the four lists of the twelve apostles. And these are the only lists of all twelve apostles. The Bible only records all the apostles four times.

## THE FOUR LISTS OF THE TWELVE APOSTLES

| Matthew 10:2-4 | Mark 3:16-19 | Luke 6:13-16 | Acts 1:13 |
|---|---|---|---|
| Now the names of the twelve apostles are these: | And He appointed the twelve: | And when the day came, He called his disciples to Him; and chose twelve of them, whom He also named as apostles: | And when they had entered, they went up to the upper room, where they were staying; that is, |
| The first Simon, who is called **Peter**, and **Andrew** his brother; and **James** the son of Zebedee, and **John** his brother; | Simon (to whom He gave the name **Peter**), and **James**, the son of Zebedee, and **John** the brother of James (to them He gave the name Boanerges, which means "Sons of Thunder"); and **Andrew**, | Simon, whom He called **Peter**, and **Andrew** his brother; and **James** and **John**; | **Peter** and **John** and **James** and **Andrew**, |
| **Philip** and **Bartholomew**; **Thomas** and **Matthew** the tax-gatherer; | and **Philip** and **Bartholomew** and **Matthew** and **Thomas**, | and **Philip** and **Bartholomew** and **Matthew** and **Thomas**, | **Philip** and **Thomas**, **Bartholomew** and **Matthew**, |
| **James** the son of Alphaeus, and **Thaddaeus**; **Simon** the Zealot, and **Judas** Iscariot, the one who betrayed Him. | and **James** the son of Alphaeus, and **Thaddaeus**, and **Simon** the Zealot; and **Judas** Iscariot, who also betrayed Him. | **James** the son of Alphaeus, and **Simon** who was called the Zealot; **Judas** the son of James, and Judas Iscariot, who became a traitor. | **James** the son of Alphaeus, and **Simon** the Zealot; and **Judas** the son of James. |

These four lists show a format. It's not a random roster of twelve people. As we can see, there are three groups within the twelve apostles. These three groups show consistently in all four lists of the twelve. The leader of each group is always the same even though the members are not.

→ Peter is always listed first. What's more, the list in Matthew 10:2 makes a point of saying Peter is the leader: "These are the names of the twelve apostles: first, Simon . . ." Peter leads the first group.

→ Philip is always listed fifth. He leads the second group.

→ James of Alphaeus is always listed ninth. James leads the third group.

Based on the listing the Bible uses, Jesus and His twelve apostles look like this:

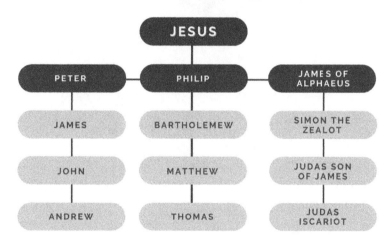

So, Jesus formatted the twelve into three groups of four. But He didn't stop there. In addition to formatting the church by formatting the leaders into three groups, He invested more direct development into the first group. What we sometimes call the "inner circle" of Peter, James, John, and Andrew got more of Jesus's time and attention than the rest of the twelve.

Notice how Jesus particularly "poured into" them:

→ The "inner circle" is always listed as the first group.

→ Jesus took the inner circle father into the Garden of Gethsemane than the others.

*"Then Jesus came with them to a place called Gethsemane,*
*and said to the disciples, 'Sit here while I go and pray over there.'*

# JESUS AND THE TWELVE

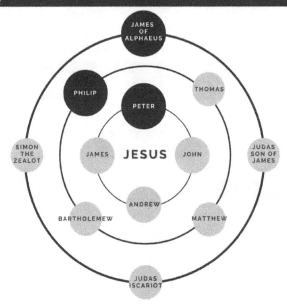

*And He took with Him Peter and the two sons of Zebedee,*
*and He began to be sorrowful and deeply distressed."*
—Matthew 26:36–37 (NKJV)

→ The inner circle witnessed the Transfiguration.

*"Now after six days Jesus took Peter, James, and John, and led them up on a*
*high mountain apart by themselves; and He was transfigured before them."*
—Mark 9:2 (NKJV)

→ Jesus only allowed the inner circle to accompany Him at the healing of
Jairus's daughter:

*"And behold, one of the rulers of the synagogue came, Jairus by name."*
—Mark 5:22 (NKJV)

> *"And He permitted no one to follow Him*
> *except Peter, James, and John the brother of James."*
> —Mark 5:37 (NKJV)

→ The inner circle wrote eight of the New Testament books and influenced a ninth (Gospel of Mark).

→ Peter is mentioned far more often (193 times) than any other disciple. He was "first."

→ John is mentioned approximately forty-six times, second-most frequently, including the phrase "whom Jesus loved."

→ Philip, at thirty-four times, is mentioned third most often. He is also the leader of the second group.

→ James of Alphaeus is likely mentioned fourth most often, at eighteen times.

Also, notice how the inner circle carried the mantle of leadership after Jesus's departure. After the church's establishment, the Apostle Paul says this:

> *"In fact, James, Peter, and John, who were known as pillars of the church."*
> —Galatians 2:9 (NLT)

The "inner circle" of the apostles, those Jesus developed to a greater degree, became the pillars, the support for the church. Jesus formed the format. Then the format supported the church as a whole.

## What Should You Do with Twelve People?

Smaller churches often underestimate their potential for kingdom impact. Here, I define a "small church" as having less than twenty attendees. What can we do with so few people? Let's take a page out of Jesus's playbook.

If you follow Jesus's strategy and have at least twelve people, you should organize them into three groups of four to maximize kingdom impact. To push your church's impact even further, the pastor uses most of their time investing in the three key leaders (of the twelve) so those three can lead the major areas of the enterprise. Remember, you first must clarify your purpose, design your plan, and do the work.

Jesus strategically used His time to expand the kingdom. What about you, pastor? With whom do you spend the majority of your time? If you follow the strategy of Jesus, you invest most of your time with your key leaders.

## On Church Governance

You, along with your church's beliefs and tradition, often determine her governance (the system by which your church is controlled and operated). Sometimes the presbytery determines church direction. Other traditions use an episcopacy undergirded by connexionalism. Elders preside over the church's functioning in some instances. In other churches, the church staff function as the elders. In still others, the elders are lay leaders who oversee the pastor, and others have the pastor functioning as one of the elders. Some churches vest the leadership in the pastor solely. And a significant number of churches follow a congregational government.

Congregationally governed churches also function in several ways, depending on what they think the whole church needs to decide or what can be handled by a person or committee. The point is, no matter your church's governance, following the strategy of Jesus will improve your effectiveness.

## Governance Makes No Guarantees

What makes churches effective is how closely they follow the strategy Jesus followed, not their governance. There are great churches that use an elder form of government. Many less-than-great churches run an elder form of government. Effective churches utilize a congregational governance. Dead and dying churches operate a congregational governance. The same can be said for an episcopacy or a presbytery or connexionalism. Governance does not guarantee effectiveness.

There's no one right model of church governance. There isn't even a prescribed biblical form of governance. We see some examples of how New Testament churches governed. We find zero mandates. *The biggest mistake you can make in governance is to think governance guarantees your effectiveness.*

Coaching sessions with pastors show many of them think that if they could just get to "having elders," their stress and frustrations would decrease and "somebody else would be there to solve all of the conflict." This thinking all but guarantees bad results. Whenever the pastor abdicates responsibility to anyone, it's going to hurt. It will cost the pastor more time and anguish in the long run, even if it feels like a relief in the short term.

On the other hand, when a pastor delegates responsibility without relinquishing overall responsibility, great things can occur. Use governance as a tool to accomplish the church's mission, not as an excuse to not solve the problems yourself.

## How to Create Your Organizational Format

Create your format to follow your mission and vision (which is part of your purpose). Once you and your key leaders get a clear, written mission for your church, then you determine your format. Your format follows your function. Your function should not follow your format.

When we sat down with a design architect to build a new worship center, his first question was, "What do you want it to do?" He did not ask how we wanted it to look or how big it would be. Those questions should only come after the function question.

The same principle applies to staffing and creating your church's format, which includes staffing. Your format also includes your building/campus, service times, small group structure, kids' ministry, youth, and preschool and adult ministry organization.

In other words, your staffing should follow your mission/vision. If your mission as a church is to worship, disciple, and evangelize, for example, your main staff should have these three key items as their major responsibilities. Any responsibility (and yes, I do mean any) should be under a staff person, and it also needs to directly support your stated mission. If you have something spinning out there that does not fit directly under your mission, it's a distraction from your mission. It may be a good thing in and of itself, but if it does not heavily support your mission, you should not be doing it. Just because it's a good thing for somebody to do does not mean your church needs to do it. Your format, as much as anything else you do, truly shows what you believe your church should be doing.

Your format determines a lot of your effectiveness. Be careful not to overlook it.

*Chapter 16*

# IMPROVE: MAKE IT FUN
# ALONG THE WAY

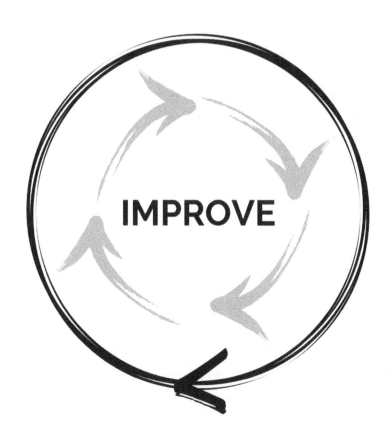

*"I get better every day."*
—Wayne Gretzky, "The greatest hockey player ever."

When I asked a newly minted pastor what shocked him most about being a pastor, he said, "I thought it would be fun." Sadly, that's a common experience for pastors not leading strategically. But it doesn't have to be that way. Ministry carries enough toils of its own without adding unnecessary angst caused by a lack of organizational effectiveness.

When you lead well, life and ministry produce fun, along with increasing kingdom impact. In addition, you can have a lot of fun in ministry. I often say, "Life's hard enough. Ministry should be fun!"

## Seven Ways to Make Ministry Fun

Here are a few things you might do to lighten the load and enjoy the ride:

*1. Plan "Hanging Out Time" with Your Leaders*

We did a shrimp boil at a neighborhood park for our staff and families. No agenda except to enjoy each other and connect relationally. Well, that's not totally true . . . I love a great shrimp boil! It was "come and go" so it wouldn't take their whole day.

Every so often, we did a staff barbecue dinner at my house. (I had the food catered so it would also be a fun time for my wife and me.) Just one random night out (with no agenda!) makes a difference for people you love and want to encourage.

*2. Make Your Office Fun*

As a pastor, the top right drawer of my office desk always held a supply of toys, mostly bouncy balls. I also had juggling balls and juggling clubs at hand. Why? Well, I like toys. And the bonus was when young parents come, they often bring their tots in tow. It's important for those little ones to see church as a fun, welcoming place. A stuffy, "no smiles allowed" pastor's office can regrettably be seen by children as representing a "No smiles God," which is not true.

The Bible tells us that "the joy of the Lord is our strength" (Nehemiah 8:10). God's joy should show up in ministry. One of my leaders told me her son wanted to bring his toys to church. She said, "You aren't supposed to have toys at church." Her son replied, "Pastor Rich has his toys at church!" The kid was right.

*3. Play Together*

After we pulled off a HUGE transition, moving from one campus to two, which included reassembling 191 (one hundred ninety-one) Sunday School classes, my staff was wiped out. The fatigue showed up at the following staff meeting. The printed agendas sat in front of each one of us. Perusing the wearied leaders around the table, I asked, "Is that putt-putt course next to Willowbrook Mall open?" Nobody knew. So we left immediately, piled into our cars, and drove there. It was closed, but I saw somebody inside the building. I beat on the door to get his attention. He graciously (with a little coaxing) let my staff play putt-putt. We had a great time and injected joy and reenergized the team. That's what I wanted.

*4. Use Meals for Fun and Connecting with Other People*

Food fascinates me. Eatables not only provide sustenance, but something as simple as a lunch together oils relationships so that everything runs more smoothly. We make it a habit (even if we missed a few) to go out to lunch as a staff at least monthly. Not only is it a good time, but when you build relationships with the leaders of ministry, you model the importance of building relationships with people in their areas of ministry. As a bonus, the food is really good!

*5. Celebrate Big Wins (or even little ones)!*

My staff and I oversaw the Spiritual Maturity area of our church. The first time our small group attendance went over 4,000 people on a Sunday, I rented a skybox at the Astrodome for the staff, just to thank and encourage them for all their work. We catered in a delicious Mexican dinner. The fajitas were delicious, but the food came in second behind the fun night of watching America's game together as a team.

*6. Use Themes to Create Fun*

Following the "Life is hard enough, ministry should be fun" principle, a good way to help keep it fun for the whole church is to envision what the next levels look like for your ministry. After you determine the vision, design themes to accomplish them. For us, one three-year blitz produced:

→ Year One: The Year of Learning (discipleship, "Get in the Game")
→ Year Two: The Year of Loving (evangelism, "All Aboard")

→ Year Three: The Year of Launching (new leaders and new classes, "Rocket Town")

## Get in the Game

We launched the Three-Year Emphasis as we rebranded the "Maturity & Ministry" area. What are the first letters of "Maturity & Ministry"? Well, M&Ms, of course. So, at our big, annual kick-off leaders' meeting, we gave tons of packages of peanut M&Ms ('cause you have to be a little nutty to lead a Bible study group) to the crowd of leaders. For the first year of the emphasis, our "Year of Learning," we chose the theme "Get in the Game." We encouraged all our leaders to wear baseball jerseys to Sunday School. We printed baseball cards featuring various church leaders. We videoed our senior pastor, Damon Shook, pitching a baseball. On the Sunday morning of the main emphasis, we cooked hamburgers on grills, beginning at 8 a.m. as people arrived at church. That was the year we went over 4,000 in Sunday School and got the skybox at the Astrodome. I cannot help but think the fun we injected contributed to the increased attendance.

## All Aboard

As believers, we want everybody to be "all aboard," and to do that, we need to share our faith with others. To increase our emphasis on evangelism, we did an "All Aboard" theme for our Bible study area. We did several things. Our staff did a video spoof of *Gilligan's Island* to promo Sunday School. Volunteers converted the welcome center into a tiki hut. Every attendee got a plastic lei to wear around their neck the Sunday morning of the event. Each Bible study class decorated their doors in some "port of call." Our Ministry Fair (letting everybody know about all the ways they could get connected) that evening distributed passports. Attendees to the Ministry Fair got their passports stamped at the various booths. Passports with a certain number of stamps got submitted for a drawing for a signed Astros jersey and other prizes. Each Bible study class or area led a particular booth. Everybody got involved. Booths served nachos, clocked how fast you could throw a baseball, and all kinds of carnival games and food. Our older ladies' class did a cakewalk. It was a lot of fun, and it increased our Bible study attendance as well as involvement in ministry.

## Rocket Town

Since we were in Houston, we used rockets and all that goes with them for the Year of Launching. Inflatables, videos of rockets lifting off, and tossing out t-shirts at our annual big leaders' meeting all helped promote launching new leaders and new classes. That's the year we developed our process of launching new classes. We started thirty new classes as well as a process for each area (preschool, children, middle school, high school, and adults). Just in the adult area alone, thirty-five adults were being trained to lead a class right after we started the thirty new classes. It was loads of fun, and we saw God do incredible things.

*7. Observe Argentina Flag Day (or create a fictitious day)*

Mark it down. When you feel draggy, so does your staff. On one of those days, my calendar said "Argentina Flag Day." I emailed my staff, apologized for my oversight at not celebrating the great flag of Argentina previously, and invited them all to lunch at a nearby eatery! Before leaving the office, I pulled several jokes from my stash. While at the restaurant, before our food arrived, each staff person read at least one joke from the cache. It was a lot of fun and brightened the day. (Hopefully, you have a folder of jokes. If not, let me know and I'll send you some.)

As you probably figured, it doesn't have to be Argentina Flag Day. You can use a real day on the calendar or just make up any kind of day, thus inventing a reason to have fun. Here are some options I just made up:

→ My Mom's Cousin Lloyd Day
→ Groundhog in My Backyard Day
→ Mongolian Barbecue Monday
→ Taco Tuesday
→ Why Am I Not Taller Wednesday
→ Therapeutic Thursday (We all need one of these once in a while.)
→ Fun Friday (You probably saw this one coming.)

Here's an idea to make ministry more enjoyable (and fun!). Pick one of these (totally make-believe) days, pick a restaurant and tell your staff you're going to celebrate that day by going to lunch together. You and your staff (and your relationships with each other) will get better.

What if you don't have a staff? I've been in that situation. In those cases, include a line item in the church's budget to pay for lunches or food catered to your house. Then, you invite your volunteer leaders to the same things I've described here. Whether it's volunteer or paid staff, you're building a team. They will love it, and so will you.

Effective pastors/leaders regularly improve themselves and the churches they lead. Many effective pastors also have fun doing it.

## Once You Start, How Do You Improve?

Congratulations! If you made it this far, your church/organization possesses a clear, workable mission. Additionally, you created a plan you can now work with. Then, you took a look at your format to determine the best structure to grease the skids of the work. If you are like organizations I help, your leaders and people are energized, seeing new growth, and excited about the future. It's exhilarating!

What happens now?

Now, we seek to improve what we are doing. Improvement comes through two primary means:

1. Planned Learning
2. Create and Manage Change

A pastor recently asked me why a particular church was dying. He knew the church used to see over 300 people regularly worshiping there. In the past, the church grew, reached people, supported missionaries, baptized a lot of people, and went to other countries to share the gospel. But in the last thirty years, she declined to the extent that it became necessary to donate the building to another ministry. What was once a hub of activity is now an empty shell. The church has less than five preschoolers and children attending.

Ironically enough, another church in our network bought the building across the street. The church across the street asked me to come and help them manage all the growth they experienced. Right across the street! That church had over sixty preschoolers and children, while this church had less than five kids on the same day.

Why did this happen?

The short answer is she did not follow the continual "Improvement" phase of the strategy of Jesus. If the dying church had regularly looked at their ministry and retooled when the changes in the community first happened, they would be more effective now.

The strategy of Jesus is not a one-time planning session. If you operate the strategy of Jesus, you will re-evaluate and retool every month for the rest of your church's life.

Additionally, you will (at least) annually take a larger look.

One of the places you look is outside your church. At least once a year, you need to revisit your mission, vision, and values. This requires looking at your Environment (what's going on outside your church) and your Capabilities (what's going on inside your church) just like you did in your initial plan.

Jesus continually planned and innovated throughout His ministry here. Effective churches do the same.

Here are two key ways to renew your church and her ministry.

## 1. Planned Learning

Through the years, I have made a regular habit of finding people who do things better and know more than I do. I then take them to breakfast, attend a seminar they lead, join an accelerator program, sign up for coaching, or pursue an additional degree. Every single interaction improves me as a leader. Very often, the improvement comes in an unexpected area I never would have been exposed to if I hadn't been chasing additional learning.

As a young youth and education pastor, a man in my church loved the Lord and oversaw $1 billion in his company. So, of course, I recruited him to be my Sunday School director. When I approached him, he said, "Why are you asking me? I don't know anything about education." I replied, "I know education. You know leadership. I need you so I can learn leadership from you."

On this day and every other day of my life, I carry leadership principles in my head that I learned from Morris Owen. As an added bonus, because Morris showed up at my leaders' meetings, other people started showing up more regularly, too.

I also used to take Paul Olson to breakfast once a month or so. He gifted me invaluable insights into leading an organization. His son was in my youth group, so what he taught me also benefited his son. I thank God for Paul's influence in my life.

Then I met a man named Denny Taylor. He was the manager of Continuous Performance Improvement at Royal Dutch Shell in Houston. He led hundreds of organizations inside Royal Dutch Shell and learned personally from some very high-profile business leaders and thinkers. He mentored me for two years. I know my eyes glazed over several times. But he never gave up. His incalculable value in my life gave direction and depth to my doctoral project, ultimately resulting in this book. So much of what I know about organizations, systems, and improvement came from him.

I could add a lot more to this list, but you get the point. You must go find these people. Some of them cross your paths every day. The great ones won't impose on you. You must make the ask. It will change your life forever if it's like my experience.

In my later years, I've had to pay quite a lot of money to get that kind of tutelage. I can tell you that every one of those cohorts, seminars, processes, accelerators, courses, podcasts, books, and personal interviews more than paid for themselves. It's usually not instant. Yet it's always exponential. Great leaders are lifetime learners. I pray God lets me join their ranks.

## 2. Create and Manage Change

For an organization to increase her effectiveness, it must infuse change regularly as well as more massive change intermittently. In the best organizations, the insiders say things like, "XYZ Church, where change is your friend." You need to change things, even if things don't need to be changed. The reason you change isn't only to improve the church. You should change things often so your people are accustomed to change.

If you are in a church that doesn't change much, it looks kind of like this:

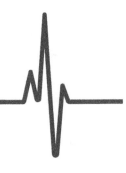

In this kind of church, any kind of change feels drastic. If your people are accustomed to seeing the same pulpit (for example) every Sunday for years on end, changing the pulpit is likely to send some of them into a tailspin. If, however, you change the pulpit (or what you wear, or how the worship center looks, or any number of things) on a regular basis, your change quotient is higher. Your church would look more like this:

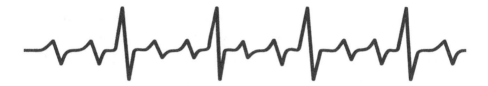

You can see how a massive change to Church A would not feel like much of a change to Church B. This is key to achieving massive effectiveness.

Leading an effective church requires two kinds of change that you, as the pastor, need to drive (and I do mean drive).

## Regular Rhythm

Even when serving as a solo pastor, you need at least a monthly rhythm of evaluation and improvement. If you don't connect at least monthly with your leaders, your church (and any organization) wanders from her mission, and things don't get accomplished. Even on a personal level, I build in accountability to keep me on track. It's even more important when working with a group of people.

A good regular rhythm looks like this:

**Annual Planning.** Here's where you take a broad look at your church's mission and your personal mission. You evaluate your effectiveness in each over the last year. Here you have a choice of three options:

1.  You stop ineffective programs/events.
2.  You add programs/events/etc. to make your mission more effective.
3.  You adjust what you are currently doing to make it more effective.

You also look at what is going on in your community and the world. You update your MAP for a longer look, at least a year. On the church level, you do this evaluation with your leaders. On a personal level, you evaluate yourself or join a cohort of like-minded individuals (not in your church) to increase your effectiveness.

**Quarterly Update.** In the past few years, I've joined a couple of groups that get together four times a year to evaluate their annual goals and update/refine them. This has helped me tremendously. I'm incorporating this additional time into my strategic routine now. Three months come and go before you know it. Can I share a secret? Sometimes I don't track my progress like I should. But I definitely check just before I know I'm meeting with my group at our quarterly meetings; I then do what I should have been doing all along. From what I've heard, the check-ins keep other people on track, too.

**Monthly Preview.** Here you plan the tactical/practical aspects of what your Annual Plan initiated. Handle details, onboard new leaders, start new groups, rearrange service times, and launch new ministries/initiatives, all within the context of your current leadership. It's extremely discouraging for your leaders to hear about a new initiative from someone else. They need to hear it from you; then, they help implement the change.

**Weekly Plan.** God created the earth with a weekly rhythm. All of us follow it. Our calendars and work weeks, for the most part, follow a weekly cycle. God also instituted a weekly regularity to worship. Personally and organizationally, you sync with life as we know it by developing a game plan for the week. Weekly, you take your annual goals and translate them into what you will accomplish this week. Keep your MAP and Annual Plan ever before you. I have mine in hand when I do my weekly planning.

**Daily Direction.** The rubber hits the road daily. God created the world day by day. Jesus prayed and sought God's favor and guidance every day. I do, too. I regularly journal. My journaling includes my prayers so I won't get distracted. Incorporated into my daily journal are my personal and organizational goals, my prayers, and my plans for the day. I also regularly ask God for wisdom.

## Intermittent Infusion

In addition to your Regular Rhythm, there are times the leader hears God speak clearly. On those occasions, you need to go for it! Even if it doesn't fit your Improvement Plan, pull the trigger and move forward! Great leaders do not hesitate to implement a new vision when they see it. Do not underestimate this. A vision can come at any time (which is why "Improve" circles the entire Organizational Strategy).

Improvement of the Plan or the Work or the Format can happen at any time. Sometimes you need to add a staff person before the next planning session. And sometimes, a volunteer leaves when it doesn't fit the schedule. Don't wait to move forward just because you are months away from setting your Annual Goals. Some of the most effective visions come outside the Regular Rhythm of your church. Avoid the tendency to skip an opportunity just because it doesn't fit anybody's rhythm of planning and evaluation. The best leaders know this and implement it when the time is right and not according to the calendar.

On the other hand, you should not just depend on a leader's "Intermittent Infusion." In addition to these intermittent times of inspiration and vision, you need a regular rhythm of evaluation and planning. The best leaders and churches vigorously follow a Regular Rhythm and implement Intermittent Infusions. God does not always work according to the schedule. Neither should you.

## Working It All Out

Sitting in a seminary classroom in my early twenties, I remember asking myself, "What happens if I do all this stuff and it doesn't work?" "Work" for me meant being effective in reaching people for Christ, impacting the community, discipling, and helping people worship God with their whole hearts.

After I landed in my first pastorate, that question became an alarming reality. It didn't "work" and hadn't for the past twenty-five years before me. I did what I knew to do: preach, pray, fast, study, share the gospel, teach, care, and counsel. But the church continued its quarter-century decline. It wasn't until I got to a place where I could use the strategy Jesus used that things really began to work.

If you want things to "work," you first must be fully "in" personally. This means you possess a clear, specific-only-to-you personal mission statement. For a pastor, your call to ministry helps form your personal mission. Then you continually increase mentally, physically, spiritually, and socially/emotionally. It starts there. But don't fall for the Pastoral Fallacy that says that's all there is to it. You also must lead organizationally.

Following the strategy of Jesus necessarily begins by leading your church (or organization) to embrace an organizational purpose. Your church's purpose includes:

a. A clear, written mission.
b. A high-definition picture of how your mission will look at a specific time in the future when it is accomplished.
c. The values by which you live and work.

With a clear purpose in hand, you next need a plan. A plan is only a plan when it includes the following seven components:

1. **Deadline:** You don't really have a target without a target date. It's the day the result must be completed. No TBDs allowed.
2. **Reviewed:** All your key leaders participated in its creation.
3. **Accountable:** Only one person is accountable for each action.
4. **Written:** Because your church cannot do what they cannot see.
5. **Measurable:** No problem can be solved until you can describe what the solution looks like in behavioral terms.
6. **Actionable:** Great plans don't include action steps beginning with tepid words like, "Review . . ." "Study . . ." "Assess . . ." Use robust, whole-hearted words like "Complete . . ." and "Implement . . ."
7. **Purpose-fulfilling:** If an action does not strongly support your purpose, don't do it. It's a deal-breaker. Don't invest time, energy, focus, or even prayers on actions that don't support what God has called you to do.

To fulfill God's call to lead organizationally, you develop a purpose and your plan. But without Work, it won't happen. It will take a lot of hard work to be effective. Laziness is craziness in Christ's kingdom. Nothing works if you don't. But just working hard doesn't guarantee results. Your work must align with your plan, and your plan must fulfill your purpose.

Even with the purpose, plan, and work, you still must format the church. You must align your organizational chart, teams, systems, processes, and budget with your purpose.

Finally, great organizations rhythmically Improve everything about the organization. They systematically evaluate and improve each area. This enables the church to consistently ratchet up its effectiveness over time.

# CONCLUSION

There is great consolation for anyone in the pastorate: the power of the strategy of Jesus is not in the leader of the church. It begins with the power of God Almighty. It continues in the process Jesus used. This necessarily includes the leader, and the good news is that "Any leader can do it." It (simply) requires a relinquishment on your part to achieve it. But by God's grace, you can lead your church effectively.

As I said at the beginning, the truth is that few churches have a strategy to incorporate the whole of what they are supposed to be doing. But now you have a well-considered strategy for what you should be doing!

You possess an overarching cohesive picture of how it all fits together. Now you can more effectively conduct worship services, preach, love people, disciple people, help the poor, share your faith, teach the Bible, and minister to your community. You have a comprehensive picture of how it can look when all the pieces are in place.

Furthermore, you know why you are growing and increasing your impact. And in areas that are less effective, you know what to do about it. Using Jesus's leadership strategy frees you to do what He called you to do. His strategy grants you the joy and fulfillment of why you entered the ministry.

This is truly great news: You are leading your church to greater effectiveness by using the strategy of Jesus. Following Jesus's leadership strategy clarifies how we need to lead the organization of the church. It systematically addresses each area within the church to evaluate and retool where needed.

Using the strategy of Jesus will not only restore your joy but the joy of those you serve.

And always remember, the strategy of Jesus works because Jesus *lived* it.

# ABOUT THE AUTHOR

In a little more than thirty years of ministry, Dr. Rich Halcombe served as solo pastor of an inner-city church (at age twenty-six), associate pastor of a suburban church (that experienced 24 percent growth year over year in the area he oversaw), and teaching pastor/pastor of spiritual formation at the seventy-fifth largest church in America, averaging around 4,500 in weekly worship on a single campus. There he oversaw 221 Bible study classes and a staff of ten full-time ministers and about 150 other employees, averaging 3,321 people in weekly Bible study. The area he led started thirty new Bible study classes and led the creation of an effective leadership development process at every level, using the leadership strategy of Jesus. He also led many other initiatives to transition to their new fifty-five-acre campus.

With his move from Texas to central Ohio, he directed a struggling network of churches. God used him to add an average of seven to fourteen churches a year to the network and create/formalize one of the most well-respected nonprofits in Columbus, Ohio. The organizations he leads experienced more than ten times growth in kingdom impact and financial increase (both to the operating income and the balance sheet).

He earned three seminary degrees (MDiv, MRE, DMin) along the way. In 2018, Rich founded leaderINCREASE to "develop leaders to achieve kingdom results, personally and organizationally" in order to make the things God taught him available to more people.

"Dr. Rich" and his wife, Tina, have been married for almost forty years, and they have several children and grandchildren, all of whom love the Lord. His favorite hobby is cooking for friends and family, whether it's in the kitchen or on his grill or barbecue smoker.

# Invitation

## Check out our personal support options!

Some leaders can read the content of this book and "get it" without further help. That's a wonderful gift. However, I was not one of those leaders. Maybe you aren't either. For me, it took personal coaching and enlisting someone to facilitate me and my staff through the process the first time. Once I experienced it, I could do it. (I still call and consult that coach, by the way).

In addition, I got a lot of help through personal coaching. There are several things I used to think that I didn't even realize were impeding my growth. It took an outside voice to help me see what I needed. If you are in a situation like I was, we can help you. Currently, we provide strategic development and coaching for hundreds of leaders a year. I also help leaders map out strategies, deal with staff issues and structure, and help them manage conflict. It's all part of operating Jesus's strategy.

**We now offer the same support to you. Contact us at www.info@strategyofjesus.com**

**To see some of the help we provide, check out www.strategyofjesus.com**

# Free Leadership Assessment

## Free Strategic Leader Assessment

Wondering what's next? As a thank you for reading the book, take this free online assessment to see how well you operate in the three necessary skill sets all leaders need: Personal, Interpersonal and Organizational.

After taking the assessment, you'll receive feedback on practical steps you can take to improve your weaker areas (and we all have them).

**Claim your free assessment now at
www.strategyofjesus.com**

# How to Contact Rich

If you are interested in increasing your skills and leading your organization to thrive, Rich can help.

For more information about keynotes and strategy workshops, contact leaderINCREASE:

Email: info@leaderincrease.com
Online: www.leaderincrease.com

Sign up for Rich's email newsletter by visiting:
www.leaderincrease.com

**Follow leaderINCREASE on social media:**

**@leaderINCREASE**

To purchase bulk copies of this book at a discount for your church or organization, please contact leaderINCREASE:
specialsales@leaderincrease.com

# ENDNOTES

1   Countrymeters.info, "Religion of the World," World population 2021 | Population clock live, accessed November 16, 2021, https://countrymeters. info/en/World#religion.

2   The term "bride" is used in reference to the church fifteen times: Matthew 9:15; 25:1, 5, 6, 10; Mark 2:19, 20; Luke 5:34, 35; John 2:9, 3:29; Revelation 18:23, 21:2, 9, 17.

3   "George Müller, Did You Know?" Christian History Institute (*Christian History* magazine) accessed November 16, 2021, https:// christianhistoryinstitute.org/magazine/article/did-you-know-mueller.

4   Müller, George, and Diana L. Matisko. *The Autobiography of George Müller.* New Kensington, PA: Whitaker House, 1985.

5   Müller and Matisko. *Autobiography of George Müller*, p. 52.

6   Müller and Matisko. *Autobiography of George Müller*, p. 54.

7   Müller and Matisko. *Autobiography of George Müller*, p. 54.

8   Müller and Matisko. *Autobiography of George Müller*, p. 60.

9   Müller and Matisko. *Autobiography of George Müller*, p. 230.

10  Müller and Matisko. *Autobiography of George Müller*, p. 232.

11  Bergeron, Josh. "Documentary to Examine Life, Work of Charles A. Cannon." *Salisbury Post*, October 9, 2017. https://www.salisburypost. com/2017/10/08/documentary-to-examine-life-work-of-charles-a-cannon/.

12  U.S. Census Bureau QuickFacts: Eden City, North Carolina. Accessed May 16, 2022. https://www.census.gov/quickfacts/fact/table/edencitynorthcarolina/BZA210220

13  "Prothesis Meaning in Bible—New Testament Greek Lexicon—New American Standard." Biblestudytools.com. Accessed May 23, 2022. https://www.biblestudytools.com/lexicons/greek/nas/prothesis.html.

14  A conversation, as referenced here, means any discourse involving Jesus's own words by my counting. If Jesus answered different people directly (even if it's within the same grouping of verses in the Bible), it's counted as different conversations (as in John 14 with Thomas, Philip, and Judas [not Iscariot]). So (again, by my count), Jesus participated in 96 conversations in Matthew, 80 in Mark, 111 in Luke, and 73 conversations in John. He acknowledged His purpose in 42 of the conversations in Matthew (42%), 19 in Mark (24%), 33 in Luke (30%), and 36 of them (49%) in the gospel of John.

15  "Nacho Libre Movie @ Omdb." Open Media Database. Accessed May 16, 2022. https://www.omdb.org/en/us/movie/9353-nacho-libre.

16  Ross, Allen P., Jerry E. Shepherd, George Schwab. "Proverbs, Ecclesiastes, Song of Songs." In *The Expositor's Bible Commentary*. United States: Zondervan Academic, 2017.

17  Gaebelein, Frank E. "Proverbs." Essay. In *The Expositor's Bible Commentary: With the New International Version of the Holy Bible*, 905. Grand Rapids, MI: Zondervan, 1992.

18  "The Water in You: Water and the Human Body." U.S. Geological Survey. Accessed November 16, 2021. https://www.usgs.gov/special-topic/water-science-school/science/water-you-water-and-human-body?qt-science_center_objects=0#qt-science_center_objects.

19  Rifkin, Harriet. "Invest in People Skills to Boost Bottom Line." Bizjournals.com. *Portland Business Journal*, June 2, 2002. https://www.bizjournals.com/portland/stories/2002/06/03/focus6.html.

20  "Biography of George Foreman." Official Website of George Foreman. https://www.georgeforeman.com/pages/biography.

21 "Did You Know?" Official Website of George Foreman. https://www. georgeforeman.com/pages/did-you-know.

22 Forleo, Marie. "The Simple Strategy That Helped Increase My Odds of Success by 42%." *CNBC: Make It.* CNBC, September 13, 2019. https://www. cnbc.com/2019/09/13/self-made-millionaire-how-to-increase-your-odds-of-success-by-42-percent-marie-forleo.html.

# A free ebook edition
# is available with the
# purchase of this book.

**To claim your free ebook edition:**

1. Visit MorganJamesBOGO.com
2. Sign your name CLEARLY in the space
3. Complete the form and submit a photo of the entire copyright page
4. You or your friend can download the ebook to your preferred device

A **FREE** ebook edition is available for you or a friend with the purchase of this print book.

CLEARLY SIGN YOUR NAME ABOVE

**Instructions to claim your free ebook edition:**
1. Visit MorganJamesBOGO.com
2. Sign your name CLEARLY in the space above
3. Complete the form and submit a photo of this entire page
4. You or your friend can download the ebook to your preferred device

## Print & Digital Together Forever.

Snap a photo

Free ebook

Read anywhere